SpringerBriefs in Computer Science

SpringerBriefs present concise summaries of cutting-edge research and practical applications across a wide spectrum of fields. Featuring compact volumes of 50 to 125 pages, the series covers a range of content from professional to academic.

Typical topics might include:

- A timely report of state-of-the art analytical techniques
- A bridge between new research results, as published in journal articles, and a contextual literature review
- A snapshot of a hot or emerging topic
- An in-depth case study or clinical example
- A presentation of core concepts that students must understand in order to make independent contributions.

Briefs allow authors to present their ideas and readers to absorb them with minimal time investment. Briefs will be published as part of Springer's eBook collection, with millions of users worldwide. In addition, Briefs will be available for individual print and electronic purchase. Briefs are characterized by fast, global electronic dissemination, standard publishing contracts, easy-to-use manuscript preparation and formatting guidelines, and expedited production schedules. We aim for publication 8–12 weeks after acceptance. Both solicited and unsolicited manuscripts are considered for publication in this series.

**Indexing: This series is indexed in Scopus, Ei-Compendex, and zbMATH **

Zhongyuan Thomas Lee

The Data Grid

A Multidisciplinary Guide to Building the Soft Infrastructure of the AI Era

 Springer

Zhongyuan Thomas Lee
Texas A&M University
College Station, TX, USA

ISSN 2191-5768   ISSN 2191-5776 (electronic)
SpringerBriefs in Computer Science
ISBN 978-3-032-25003-2   ISBN 978-3-032-25004-9 (eBook)
https://doi.org/10.1007/978-3-032-25004-9

This Springer imprint is published by the registered company Springer Nature Switzerland AG
The registered company address is: Gewerbestrasse 11, 6330 Cham, Switzerland

Preface

We are living in the era of Industry 4.0 and entering the transition toward Industry 5.0. Artificial intelligence has emerged as the visible protagonist of this transformation. Its capabilities expand at unprecedented speed, its applications proliferate across sectors, and its influence extends more broadly than any single technological wave in previous industrial revolutions.

Yet beneath this rapid front-end expansion lies a quieter but more fundamental layer: data.

AI may command attention, but data forms its foundation. Without structured, reliable, and governed data systems, intelligent applications cannot achieve stable and sustained performance. Across industries, a recurring pattern has become evident: the development and deployment of AI systems are accelerating faster than the maturation of the data infrastructures that support them. In many cases, industrial implementation has outpaced systematic academic theory, widening the gap between practical adoption and disciplined engineering principles.

The central challenge we face today is not whether we possess sufficient data, but whether our data systems are stable, coherent, and trustworthy. Heterogeneous, fragmented, semantically inconsistent, and sometimes contaminated data environments directly degrade AI outputs. Many enterprise AI initiatives fall short of expectations not because algorithms are inadequate, but because the underlying data foundation lacks structural robustness.

If data truly serves as the base of AI, it must be treated as infrastructure rather than merely as an asset. Infrastructure carries defining engineering properties: stability, generality, scalability, reliability, and lifecycle continuity. Applications built upon infrastructure inherit these properties. Conversely, instability at the foundational layer inevitably propagates upward.

Data engineering as a practical discipline originally emerged from computer engineering and software engineering. This origin shaped its early focus on computational efficiency, code implementation, and system performance. While this foundation has been essential to the growth of data systems, it has also, to some extent, constrained integration with broader engineering disciplines. As data volumes expand, AI systems proliferate, and digital twins become pervasive across industries, data systems are no longer confined to computational or software problems. They are evolving into cross-organizational, cross-platform, and lifecycle-spanning structural systems.

When data becomes the carrier of digital twins—continuously mapping and synchronizing physical and virtual environments—its infrastructure can no longer be designed within a narrow computational perspective. It increasingly exhibits systemic characteristics similar to traditional infrastructures such as electrical grids and communication networks. This evolution is not incidental; it reflects the natural progression of data from localized technical tooling to distributed, infrastructure-scale systems. From first principles, data infrastructure shares deep structural similarities with established engineering infrastructures. The lifecycle of data—from generation to transformation to consumption—resembles the lifecycle of electrical energy from generation to transmission, distribution, and end use. The progressive semantic enrichment of data mirrors the layered encapsulation mechanisms found in communication protocol stacks. These parallels are not superficial metaphors; they reveal transferable engineering doctrines. If data systems are indeed evolving from heterogeneous local structures into large-scale distributed infrastructure grids, then methodologies from systems engineering, industrial engineering, reliability engineering, and risk management become not only relevant but necessary. Determinism, fault isolation, boundary definition, load regulation, lifecycle segmentation, and governance control are not new engineering challenges. What is new is their reinterpretation within software-defined and distributed data environments.

This book adopts a cross-disciplinary perspective grounded in infrastructure thinking. It integrates theoretical reasoning with engineering case studies to explore how data systems in AI-native organizations can be constructed as stable, scalable, and semantically governed foundations. Rather than focusing on specific tools or transient architectural patterns, the discussion centers on structural principles that remain invariant under scale. The objective is not to diminish the importance of AI, but to clarify its operational boundaries. Intelligent systems can operate reliably only within disciplined data environments. By re-establishing data infrastructure as a structured, layered, observable, and governable engineering domain, it becomes possible to narrow the widening gap between rapid AI adoption and foundational system stability.

In the AI era, data is no longer a passive resource. It functions as continuously flowing soft infrastructure. The purpose of this book is to formalize how such infrastructure can be engineered with rigor, cross-disciplinary coherence, and long-term resilience.

College Station, USA   Zhongyuan Thomas Lee

Acknowledgments Here I especially thank my wife Minjoo (Tina) and my sons Daniel and David, for their patience with me while I was absent so often due to work and writing.

I also thank my Ph.D. advisor, Prof. Hamid R. Parsaei, for his unwavering academic support and guidance.

And thanks to Compass, Capital One, CVS Health, Verizon, and LSIS Korea— these companies, one after another, shaped my career and let me turn theory into real engineering work, the hands-on path I couldn't have walked without them.

Competing Interests The author has no competing interests to declare that are relevant to the content of this manuscript.

Contents

About the Author

Zhongyuan Thomas Lee (formerly known as Zhongyuan Li) is a doctoral researcher in Multidisciplinary Engineering at Texas A&M University, College Station, specializing in Industry 4.0/5.0 systems, digital twins, and AI-ready data infrastructures. Drawing upon cross-disciplinary methodologies from industrial engineering, systems engineering, computer science, and data engineering, he focuses on designing scalable, intelligent, infrastructure-oriented data systems that support reliable and trustworthy AI deployment at scale. With over fifteen years of professional experience as a data engineer, his career spans critical infrastructure sectors including power grids (LSIS Korea, State Grid China), telecommunications (Verizon), finance (Capital One), and health care (CVS Health). He currently serves at Compass, where he designs and architects enterprise-scale data infrastructure initiatives. He has published over twenty-five peer-reviewed papers, including works with Springer, SCI-indexed journals, and award-winning conference publications. This book integrates his industry experience with multidisciplinary research to provide a rigorous yet practical framework for building AI-ready data infrastructures.

Chapter 1
Data as Soft Infrastructure in the AI Era

Abstract This introductory chapter establishes the conceptual foundation for treating data as infrastructure in the AI era. It argues that the reliability and sustainability of intelligent systems depend not only on algorithmic performance but on the stability, observability, and governance of the underlying data environment. Drawing from established infrastructure disciplines, the chapter introduces the concept of the Data Grid as a software-defined infrastructure designed to support continuous data generation, validation, transformation, and consumption. Four engineering principles—structural determinism, lifecycle discipline, system observability, and explicit AI boundary design—are presented as foundational properties. The chapter outlines the methodological structure of the book and frames data infrastructure as a cross-disciplinary engineering domain rather than a collection of tools or architectural patterns.

Keyword Data infrastructure · Soft infrastructure · Data Grid

The development of modern industrial society can be understood, at its core, as the history of infrastructure evolution. The First Industrial Revolution was not merely a mechanical breakthrough; it brought coal- and steam-powered transportation networks that fundamentally reshaped physical distance and economic connectivity. The Second Industrial Revolution established universal electrical grids, transforming energy from a localized luxury into a ubiquitous and standardized utility. The Third Industrial Revolution introduced semiconductor computing and global-scale internet connectivity, forming the digital communication fabric on which contemporary economies and societies now depend.

Today, we stand in the midst of Industry 4.0—an era defined by data, connectivity, and AI—and we are rapidly moving toward Industry 5.0, where intelligent systems must coexist with human-centered, resilient, and sustainable industrial objectives. This is an age characterized by the convergence of autonomous intelligence and global-scale data production. In such a context, it is no longer sufficient to build systems that merely transport, store, and process data. The infrastructural imperative has changed. We must instead treat data as an infrastructure-grade object and design data systems from an infrastructure perspective: with explicit norms, enforceable standards, and engineered stability. Data—now a foundational substrate of enterprise intelligence—must be governed with the same rigor historically applied to power grids, transportation networks, and communication systems. The central premise of this book is that the AI era requires a new category of soft infrastructure: a Data Grid.

In this book, the Data Grid does not refer to geopolitical sovereignty, regulatory sovereignty, or data-jurisdiction sovereignty. Rather, it denotes operational infrastructure sovereignty: the ability of a data infrastructure to operate reliably, observably, and predictably under continuously evolving workload, scale, organizational complexity, and business requirements. Data infrastructure is not identical to traditional physical infrastructure. It is software-defined, continuously mutable, and increasingly shaped—directly and indirectly—by AI-assisted agents and automation. These realities introduce new properties and new risks. Accordingly, this book defines a Data Grid as soft infrastructure with four core engineering properties:

1. Structural Determinism: The design and operation of data must follow strict, enforceable paradigms. Determinism here does not mean that every outcome is identical under all circumstances; it means that the structural behavior of the grid—its schema topology, lineage reconstruction, transformation contracts, and enforcement mechanisms—is reproducible within defined control boundaries. This is the primary defense against "data swamps," where uncontrolled heterogeneity turns repositories into liabilities.
2. Infrastructure Observability: Every critical process in the grid must be externally inspectable, controllable, and auditable. Observability is achieved not through ad hoc dashboards alone, but through structured, queryable metadata that exposes system state, execution behavior, policy enforcement, and failure conditions as first-class infrastructure signals.
3. Universality and Interoperability: A Data Grid must be designed for interconnection, extensibility, and cross-domain reuse. Its standards and contracts should support plug-and-play integration across teams, departments, and organizations—preventing the formation (or persistence) of data silos and enabling scalable ecosystem growth without repeated reinvention.
4. Boundary Engineering for AI-Augmented Construction: Unlike traditional infrastructure, modern data infrastructure can be directly operated on by AI and automation—generating code, orchestrating workflows, proposing transformations, and even producing governance artifacts. The critical engineering question is therefore not whether to use AI, but where the boundary lies: what must remain deterministic, verifiable, and human-governed; what may be delegated to AI within bounded control surfaces; and what safety mechanisms are required to ensure recoverability when probabilistic behavior fails.

With these principles as the foundation, this book explores how to construct data as soft infrastructure—systematically, rigorously, and operationally—rather than as fragmented project artifacts. The remainder of the introduction outlines the book's approach and structure.

1.1 The Paradigm Shift: From Resource to Infrastructure

Across every major industrial transition, technology has acted as the visible catalyst, but infrastructure has determined whether that technology could deliver sustained, enterprise-scale impact. Steam engines required railway networks to connect markets. Electricity required standardized transmission grids for reliable, ubiquitous delivery. Digital economies required elastic cloud computing to power global applications. Artificial Intelligence is now the next catalytic force—yet its long-term reliability and value at enterprise scale will depend primarily on the maturity of the infrastructure that enables intelligence to be generated, distributed, validated, and operationalized sustainably.

Historically, data has been treated as a resource: a valuable input collected and shaped ad hoc for specific projects, analyses, or business needs. In the early eras of databases, data warehouses, and even initial data lakes, usage was driven largely by immediate purpose and perceived value. Individual teams, projects, companies—and often individual engineers—applied their own conventions, formats, pipelines, and quality thresholds. The prevailing mindset was outcome-oriented: extract value where possible, and tolerate variability as long as the final deliverable was produced. As data volumes exploded and platforms evolved—from relational stores to big data systems, data lakes, and lakehouses—expectations began to shift. Organizations started scrutinizing data not only for immediate delivery, but for systemic properties: consistency, discoverability, lineage traceability, and long-term usability. Yet many environments remained fragmented pipeline ecosystems—brittle, opaque, and prone to silent drift.

The AI era, particularly the rise of large-scale models and enterprise generative systems, has accelerated this shift dramatically. These systems are voracious consumers of data: they require vast quantities, continuous freshness, and—critically—stable, trustworthy supply. Feeding AI is no longer a one-time batch problem; it requires an ongoing, reliable flow akin to a utility. Insufficient or unstable data starves model performance; erratic quality contaminates outputs, causing hallucinations, biases, or failures that cascade into operational and strategic decisions.

In practice, enterprise AI often inherits the opposite: massive volumes combined with persistent instability. Data swamps repeatedly emerge—repositories where volume outpaces governance and potential assets become liabilities. Data silos persist and intensify across departments, systems, and legacy boundaries. Silos block unified views, slow integration, and make consistent quality and traceability nearly impossible. The result is not only undernourished models, but polluted ecosystems where poor data in one domain contaminates downstream intelligence and erodes organizational trust. The root causes extend beyond tooling limitations or inconsistent developer experience. Norms and standards for data construction are abundant—many quite advanced—yet fragmentation endures. Systems may nominally comply with schemas or governance frameworks, but often only in name, lacking genuine enforcement or alignment. The deeper issue is a misaligned foundational perspective: many practices still stem from a "resource" worldview—project-specific value and tactical optimization—rather than a coherent, systemic one.

Treating data as infrastructure changes the design target. Infrastructure thinking demands norms anchored in invariant principles—reliability, observability, determinism within boundaries, and failure isolation—rather than proliferating tactical details. Every standard, contract, and boundary must be justified by its contribution to the grid's stability and predictability. Without this shift, specifications multiply chaotically, enforcement becomes inconsistent, and the system devolves into the heterogeneity it seeks to escape. Data infrastructure-ization yields three strategic advantages:

1. First, plug-and-play integration: As standardized interfaces in power systems allow seamless connection, a mature Data Grid enables new applications—AI agents, analytics tools, governance services, and shared models—to "plug in" without rebuilding pipelines, converting formats, or re-aligning semantics from scratch. Integration costs drop, innovation cycles accelerate, and the ecosystem becomes genuinely composable.
2. Second, universality: A Data Grid as soft infrastructure aims for standards independent of industry, geography, or department. This addresses a structural defect in current data systems: extreme heterogeneity across industries and within enterprises. Structural differences drive exponential collaboration costs, recurring semantic conflicts, and non-reusable governance rules, ultimately trapping enterprise AI in fragmented foundations. Infrastructure thinking seeks the deepest common denominators—analogous to a universal substrate layer—so that diverse organizations can interconnect under unified deterministic boundaries.
3. Third, interoperability and interconnection: The trajectory of data is clear: enterprises will retain proprietary internal data, yet data systems will inevitably interconnect across organizations and ecosystems—supporting sharing, exchange, marketplaces, and cross-domain learning. Without a universal, deterministic, pluggable substrate, interconnection incurs astronomical conversion costs—or becomes impossible. With it, enterprises can participate securely and controllably in data-flow ecosystems and unlock data's role as a true factor of production.

For these reasons, the transition from data-as-resource to data-as-soft-infrastructure is not merely a technical evolution; it is an enterprise imperative. If organizations remain trapped in fragmented governance and resource thinking, enterprise AI will remain constrained by swamps, silos, and structural heterogeneity, unable to achieve reliable, efficient, sustainable intelligent production. The Data Grid proposed in this book is designed precisely to meet this need—transforming data from scattered artifacts into a reliable, controllable, and sustainable foundation for the enterprise intelligence era.

1.2 The Engineering Implication: A Shared Cross-Disciplinary Essence

Despite the rapid evolution of data technologies, a critical paradox persists. Data is often called the "new oil," yet the industrial-scale refineries, standardized transmission protocols, and high-reliability frameworks required to treat it as true infrastructure remain largely absent. Many contemporary data environments are still pipeline ecosystems—brittle, opaque, and vulnerable to cascading failure.

This book deliberately steps beyond the traditional confines of computer science by adopting a multidisciplinary engineering perspective. From first principles, challenges such as flow stability, system reliability, uncertainty management, and failure containment are invariant across engineering domains. The central thesis is that data grids and physical infrastructure grids—electrical transmission networks, process-control systems, and other large-scale engineered systems—share a deep structural essence. Load balancing and fault isolation in power grids resemble governance enforcement, metadata flow control, lineage reconstruction, and quality containment in data platforms. Safety–critical systems rely on explicit failure domains, redundancy, deterministic control surfaces, and lifecycle observability—requirements that are structurally analogous to what enterprise-scale AI demands from its data foundation.

Why insist on cross-disciplinary migration? Because prior industrial infrastructures have matured through decades—and in some cases centuries—of operational refinement. Electrical, civil, industrial, and systems engineering have developed battle-tested methodologies for determinism, redundancy, safety factors, and resilient operation. These methods are not merely inspirational; they are transferable. Accordingly, multidisciplinary integration in this book operates on two tightly coupled layers:

1. Methodological Layer: synthesizing governing design principles across disciplines to define how data infrastructure should be structured, reasoned about, and evolved.
2. Engineering Execution Layer: translating proven operational practices into practical, repeatable implementations for data engineering.

Through concrete case studies, the book demonstrates how cross-disciplinary knowledge transfer can elevate data infrastructure engineering from an architectural philosophy to a rigorous, reproducible discipline capable of sustaining trustworthy enterprise AI.

1.3 System-Of-Systems: Digital Twins for Data Infrastructure

At the heart of this transformation lies a guiding engineering idea: data infrastructure is a system of systems.

Digital twins were originally applied to equipment and industrial processes, creating computable mirrors for monitoring, simulation, optimization, and predictive maintenance. In the AI era, the same logic must extend to the infrastructure that produces, moves, and governs data. If we aim to represent the world through data, we cannot exempt the data infrastructure itself from representation. This mirrors a foundational pattern in mature infrastructures—especially power systems. The primary system manages the physical flow of energy. The secondary system—SCADA networks, protection relays, monitoring, and control layers—collects real-time data, observes state, enforces stability, detects anomalies, and triggers automated responses. Without the secondary layer, the primary grid is opaque; with it, the grid becomes observable, controllable, and resilient.

Data infrastructure must follow the same logic. We must digitize—create digital twins of—not only raw data flows, but also pipelines, transformation logic, governance rules, orchestration mechanisms, quality contracts, lineage records, failure modes, and operational state. This produces a comprehensive, self-referential digital twin of the infrastructure layer itself. The payoff is practical and immediate:

1. End-to-end observability and automated remediation through introspective access to metadata, policy execution, failure signals, and lineage.
2. Significant cost reduction by reducing firefighting, preventing cascading failures, and improving recoverability.
3. Accelerated resilience and scalability through self-aware control loops that adapt to load and organizational change without proportional increases in human oversight.

Without infrastructure datafication and standardization, data systems remain opaque and structurally heterogeneous—each an isolated artifact shaped by local practice. By fully embracing digital twins for the infrastructure layer, we establish the necessary substrate for a truly sovereign, observable, and autonomously reliable Data Grid.

1.4 The Reliability Boundary: Deterministic Infrastructure in the AI Era

Traditional infrastructures are engineered on deterministic control principles: predictable, repeatable behavior under defined conditions. AI systems, by contrast, operate through probabilistic inference. While often empirically accurate, they cannot guarantee correctness across every state or rare edge condition. The question, therefore, is not whether to use AI. The decisive question is: where is the boundary?

Infrastructure-grade systems must remain controllable, measurable, auditable, and recoverable. From an engineering and risk-management perspective, imperfect outputs can be acceptable in bounded contexts—provided the process is testable, replaceable, and failure is containable. White-box mechanisms can be incorporated into engineered systems because they can be validated and recovered. Black-box behavior that cannot be tested, drifts unpredictably over time, and cannot be replaced or controlled becomes dangerous at infrastructure scale. Boundary engineering follows directly:

1. Structural substrates—schema topology, lineage, governance contracts, core enforcement behavior—must remain deterministic, mechanically verifiable, externally auditable, and human-governed.
2. Bounded functional domains—code generation, transformation synthesis, optimization—may be AI-augmented, but only behind deterministic validation gates, with circuit breakers, rollback points, audit trails, and safe fallback paths.

In this architecture, AI becomes a bounded co-processor—powerful within engineered control surfaces, but never permitted to compromise structural integrity.

1.5 The Implementation Path: The Roadmap to the Data Grid

This book is organized as a disciplined progression from historical necessity to engineered execution:

1. Paradigm Shift (This chapter and Chaps. 2 and 3): Establishes why data must be reframed as the foundational substrate of the AI era, and defines the core components of data infrastructure and their respective responsibilities.
2. Architectural Blueprint (Chapter 4): Presents the book's central framework: a principled blueprint for Data Grid construction grounded in lifecycle thinking, semantic elevation, system self-description, and explicit AI boundary engineering.
3. Construction Methods and Case Studies (Chapters 5–10): Translates the blueprint into implementation. Each chapter focuses on a critical component of data infrastructure, showing how principles become operational mechanisms, and demonstrating reproducible case studies.
4. The Future of Data Infrastructure (Chapter 11): Synthesizes design insights into a forward-looking outlook on the evolution of soft infrastructure for enterprise intelligence.

This book is written for both strategic decision-makers seeking a long-term infrastructural North Star and technical practitioners requiring a rigorous, repeatable methodology. We invite the reader to move beyond viewing data as isolated datasets or project artifacts, and instead recognize it as the soft infrastructure that will sustain the next century of machine civilization.

1.6 Further Reading

To situate the historical, engineering, and governance foundations of the Soft Infrastructure Era articulated in this introduction—spanning industrial grid evolution, data as infrastructure, multidisciplinary transfer, digital twins, and AI trust boundaries—the following peer-reviewed works and authoritative technical publications provide rigorous theoretical grounding and complementary perspectives.

- Edwards, P. N. (2003). Infrastructure and modernity: Force, time, and social organization in the history of sociotechnical systems. Modernity and Technology, MIT Press.

  - Annotation: Edwards' historical analysis of large-scale sociotechnical systems (including electricity, telecommunications, and computing) frames infrastructure not merely as a technical substrate but as an organizing logic of modern society. His work provides conceptual grounding for understanding data grids as a new layer of infrastructural modernity rather than as isolated technological artifacts.

- Hughes, T. P. (1983). Networks of Power: Electrification in Western Society, 1880–1930. Johns Hopkins University Press.

  - Annotation: A foundational study of electrical grid development, demonstrating how technical standardization, institutional alignment, and system integration enabled large-scale electrification. The parallels to data infrastructure—particularly regarding standardization, interoperability, and reliability enforcement—are structurally instructive.

- Saltzer, J. H., Reed, D. P., & Clark, D. D. (1984). End-to-end arguments in system design. ACM Transactions on Computer Systems, 2(4), 277–288.

  - Annotation: Introduces the end-to-end principle in distributed system design, clarifying where functionality and trust should reside within layered architectures. This work provides foundational insight for defining deterministic boundaries and responsibility layers in AI-augmented data infrastructure.

- Weiser, M. (1991). The computer for the twenty-first century. Scientific American, 265(3), 94–104.

  - Annotation: Although focused on ubiquitous computing, Weiser's vision of pervasive, embedded computation anticipates the "Everything is Data" paradigm. It frames computation and data as ambient infrastructure rather than discrete tools—supporting the conceptual expansion of data as soft infrastructure.

- Batini, C., & Scannapieco, M. (2016). Data and Information Quality: Dimensions, Principles and Techniques. Springer.

    - Annotation: A rigorous treatment of data quality engineering, including determinism, traceability, and lifecycle governance. It complements the operational determinism and observability requirements central to sovereign data grids.

- Chen, M., Mao, S., & Liu, Y. (2014). Big data: A survey. Mobile Networks and Applications, 19(2), 171–209. Annotation: Surveys the evolution from data storage to large-scale data ecosystems. Highlights systemic challenges in scalability, heterogeneity, and reliability—motivating the shift from pipeline thinking to infrastructural thinking.
- Gorton, I., Klein, J., & Nord, R. (2019). Architectural tactics for distributed AI systems. IEEE Software, 36(3), 34–42.

    - Annotation: Discusses reliability, fault isolation, and architectural strategies for AI-enabled distributed systems. Provides technical grounding for defining explicit engineering trust boundaries when integrating probabilistic components into infrastructure-grade systems.

- IEEE (2021). IEEE 7000–2021: Model Process for Addressing Ethical Concerns During System Design. IEEE Standards Association.

    - Annotation: Establishes formal processes for embedding governance, accountability, and risk mitigation into system engineering. Relevant to defining enforceable trust boundaries and governance contracts within AI-integrated data grids.

- Monostori, L. (2014). Cyber-physical production systems: Roots, expectations and R&D challenges. Procedia CIRP, 17, 9–13.

    - Annotation: Examines cyber-physical integration in Industry 4.0, emphasizing deterministic control, system-of-systems thinking, and resilience. Offers conceptual continuity between industrial infrastructure engineering and modern data infrastructure design.

- Brunton, S. L., & Kutz, J. N. (2019). Data-Driven Science and Engineering. Cambridge University Press.

    - Annotation: Bridges traditional engineering principles with data-driven modeling and AI systems. Particularly useful for understanding how deterministic engineering frameworks can coexist with probabilistic learning systems under defined control regimes.

- NIST (2023). Artificial Intelligence Risk Management Framework (AI RMF 1.0). National Institute of Standards and Technology.

- Annotation: Provides a structured approach to measuring, managing, and governing AI risks in operational systems. Offers practical guidance for implementing measurable, auditable, and recoverable AI boundaries within infrastructure contexts.

- IEA (2024). Electricity 2024 – Analysis and Forecast to 2026. International Energy Agency.

  - Annotation: Analyzes how data centers and AI workloads increasingly influence grid stability and planning. Illustrates the reciprocal relationship between physical infrastructure and intelligence infrastructure—underscoring the necessity of reliability and deterministic control at scale.

Together, these works reinforce the core thesis of this book: that the evolution from data as resource to data as sovereign soft infrastructure is not merely technological but infrastructural, multidisciplinary, and fundamentally engineering-driven. They provide historical precedent, theoretical structure, and risk-aware governance principles for constructing Data Grids capable of sustaining trustworthy enterprise-scale intelligence.

Chapter 2
The Foundations of Soft Data Infrastructure

Abstract This chapter examines the structural challenges underlying large-scale AI deployment. It argues that the primary constraint is not data volume but data stability, semantic coherence, and governance maturity. The chapter formalizes the reclassification of data from a project-level asset to an infrastructure layer and analyzes the limitations of approaches rooted solely in software engineering traditions. By integrating principles from systems and reliability engineering, it identifies core infrastructure requirements, including standardization, decoupling, measurability, scalability, and lifecycle segmentation. The chapter differentiates the proposed infrastructure-oriented methodology from prevailing paradigms such as Data Mesh and Lakehouse architectures, establishing the theoretical basis for the architectural framework developed in subsequent chapters.

Keyword Soft data infrastructure · Data stability · Systems engineering · Reliability engineering · Data governance maturity · Infrastructure-oriented methodology

2.1   From Data Exhaust to Data Infrastructure

Building on the infrastructural paradigm introduced in the Introduction, we now examine how data evolved operationally from a passive exhaust to an engineered infrastructure layer.

In the traditional "Digital Age," systems were primarily logic-driven under deterministic software execution models. Their central purpose was to digitize business processes through code. Human engineers acted as the principal architects and implementers, translating organizational intuition into millions of lines of deterministic instructions. In this environment, data was treated largely as a passive byproduct of system execution—a secondary artifact or "exhaust" emitted from transactional processes. It was stored in localized, siloed databases, primarily for auditing and retrospective reporting. Application logic dominated system behavior, while data functioned as a supporting execution artifact rather than a structural backbone.

The rise of Cloud Computing and Big Data technologies marked the first major paradigm shift. As storage and computation became inexpensive and elastic, the industry transitioned from simple digitization toward data-driven applications. Organizations began mining vast volumes of information to feed back into production systems, improving efficiency and supporting increasingly complex commercial decision-making. This era triggered an unprecedented explosion in global data production. Yet, just as the industry struggled to balance data quantity and data quality, the sudden emergence of Generative AI redefined the stakes almost overnight. Modern AI models demonstrate an accelerating demand for high-quality, structured data. In many cases, they have already absorbed a significant portion of publicly available digital knowledge. While some commentators suggest that we are approaching a "data exhaustion" point, the reality is more nuanced. The crisis we face is not one of raw volume, but of quality, structure, and governance integrity.

The magnitude of this transition becomes evident when we distinguish between aggregate data generation and specialized data consumption. Over the past decade, global data volume has increased at an extraordinary pace, reflecting the triumph of mass digitization and ubiquitous connectivity. However, this aggregate growth obscures a more aggressive internal dynamic within artificial intelligence systems. The resource appetite of frontier AI models has expanded at a rate that outpaces traditional technological scaling patterns. While total global data production continues to rise steadily, the specific pools of high-quality training data are being consumed at an accelerating rate. This creates a critical scarcity paradox: in a world saturated with raw data, the supply of high-quality, policy-compliant, structurally reliable training data is becoming increasingly constrained.

More importantly, whether we consider general-purpose foundation models or enterprise-grade AI applications, data is inherently a double-edged sword. High-quality, well-structured, properly governed data—when amplified by AI—can generate extraordinary value. It enables predictive accuracy, operational optimization, new forms of automation, and even entirely novel business models. However, poor-quality, inconsistent, biased, or weakly governed data can contaminate the entire ecosystem. Errors propagate. Hallucinations amplify. Decisions degrade. Risk compounds across interconnected systems. The result is not isolated failure, but a cascading reaction—where corrupted inputs lead to systemic instability across models, processes, and organizational trust. It is therefore unrealistic to declare that we will "eliminate bad data." No infrastructure—physical or digital—can guarantee absolute purity. Power grids cannot eliminate all faults; transportation systems cannot eliminate all accidents. The true engineering objective is different.

Our goal is to place uncertainty inside a controllable cage. We seek to make data processes controllable, knowable, observable, and durable. We aim to constrain variability within defined boundaries, to detect anomalies before they cascade, and to ensure that failure remains isolated rather than systemic. These are not aesthetic preferences; they are infrastructure-level requirements. Just as electrical systems rely on standards, redundancy, circuit breakers, and protective relays to confine risk, data infrastructure must establish enforceable control boundaries that make uncertainty measurable and manageable. To achieve this, we must move beyond viewing data management as a localized technical function. Instead, we adopt an Industrial Engineering perspective and propose a fundamental shift in consciousness: treating the chaotic, fragmented landscape of data processing as a unified infrastructure.

Historically, every industrial revolution followed a similar trajectory—moving from early disorder to standardized stability. Consider the evolution of the electrical grid. It began with the fierce "War of Currents" between AC and DC systems, eventually converging on harmonized voltages and frequencies that power the world today. Similarly, the telecommunications era saw a proliferation of competing protocols before converging on standardized communication frameworks that enabled stable global information exchange. Data infrastructure now faces comparable large-scale coordination challenges under reliability and control constraints. Like electrons in a power grid or signals in a communication network, data is an invisible operational flow that must be engineered and governed through observable interfaces and explicit control mechanisms. The grids that carry electricity and the networks that transmit signals are functionally analogous to the tables, storage layers, schemas, and pipelines that transport and transform data. Yet a crucial distinction remains. The carriers of power and telecommunications are forms of Hard Infrastructure—composed of physical cables, transformers, and hardware systems. The carrier of data, by contrast, is a Soft Infrastructure.

This Soft Infrastructure is an invisible grid residing in the cloud. It is defined not by copper or fiber, but by standardized protocols, metadata schemas, orchestration logic, validation contracts, and autonomous control mechanisms. It is the intangible but engineered substrate that ensures intelligence can flow reliably, observably, and sustainably across systems.

The transition from data exhaust to data infrastructure is therefore not simply a technological evolution. It is an infrastructural reclassification. Data is no longer the residue of logic; it is the grid upon which logic, AI, and enterprise intelligence now depend.

2.2 First Principles and Engineering Requirements of Soft Infrastructure

To define the foundational requirements of a Data Soft Infrastructure, we must start with first principles by examining the enduring characteristics that have made physical infrastructures reliable utilities for over a century. A system only earns the status of "infrastructure" when it evolves from a specialized tool into a universal, always-available utility. This transition demands certain baseline conditions and defining features: invisibility to users (reliable enough to fade into the background), universality (applicable across domains without customization), resilience (self-protecting against failures), measurability (trackable for optimization), decoupling (layered for specialization), and scalability (open for growth). These are not optional; they are the non-negotiable thresholds that separate ad-hoc tools from civilization-scale systems.

By distilling the invariant traits of mature infrastructures—such as electrical grids, transportation networks, and telecommunications—we can identify the essential engineering requirements that data environments must adopt to achieve comparable maturity. For data to become true infrastructure, it must undergo a profound shift: from a reactive, project-specific resource (e.g., siloed datasets mined on demand) to a proactive, systemic utility (e.g., a metered, standardized flow that powers intelligence workloads predictably). This transformation involves moving away from artisanal data handling—manual cleaning, ad-hoc pipelines, and inconsistent governance— toward industrialized refinement: automated ingestion, enforcement, and delivery at scale. Without this shift, data remains a bottleneck; with it, it becomes an enabler of sustainable AI-driven productivity.

These requirements are not analogies; they are transferable first principles adapted to distributed, software-defined realities:

- Universal Standardization (The Common Voltage): Infrastructure must enforce baseline consistency to enable interoperability. Just as electrical grids mandate unified voltage and frequency standards to ensure any device plugs in safely, data infrastructure demands comprehensive consistency at ingestion—unified formats, schemas, timestamps, granularity, and semantic conventions. Chaos at inges-tion—seemingly trivial—propagates catastrophic inconsistencies downstream, much like unstable voltage frying appliances. In practice, this requires mandatory schema-on-read/write enforcement, canonical data models, and ingestion-time validation contracts to create a "common voltage" for all downstream processing. The shift for data: from variable, team-specific formats to enforce enterprise-wide standards, eliminating "format wars" that plague legacy systems.
- Structural Reliability and Invisibility: Infrastructure's core feature is its invisi-bility—we notice it only in failure. This "always-on" reliability is engineered through automated resilience: circuit breakers, self-healing protocols, redundant paths, and isolation mechanisms prevent localized faults from cascading. In data, invisibility means rigorous, automated quality controls, proactive drift detec-tion, lineage-based alerting, and autonomous remediation (e.g., circuit breakers that halt propagation of tainted data). The goal: downstream consumers experi-ence uninterrupted, trustworthy data flow without ever thinking about the under-lying grid. For data's transformation: from fragile, high-maintenance pipelines (requiring constant manual fixes) to self-sustaining systems that operate with utility-like continuity, measured through incident frequency, time-to-detection, time-to-recovery, and downstream impact containment, turning visibility into a diagnostic tool rather than a daily chore.
- Systemic Decoupling and Specialization: A key condition is layered indepen-dence: infrastructure decouples generation from transmission, distribution, and consumption to allow focused innovation without systemic risk. In data, we must enforce healthy separation between ingestion/landing, cleansing/normalization, modeling/semantic layering, and application consumption. Clear domain bound-aries—via data contracts, lineage tracking, and modular pipelines—enable

specialists (e.g., data engineers on modeling, ML teams on features) to innovate within a robust, shared framework, avoiding monolithic pipelines that couple everything together. The required shift: data moves from entangled, end-to-end scripts (where one change breaks everything) to modular, contract-bound layers, fostering specialization and reducing blast radius of errors.

- Measurability and Net Metering: Infrastructure must be fully quantifiable for optimization and accountability—every unit (e.g., kilowatt-hour) tracked, valued, and billed. For data, this shifts it from "free-flowing exhaust" to a metered, valued asset, requiring end-to-end observability: precise tracking of volume, velocity, quality, lineage, cost, and usage via governance frameworks and lineage graphs. Just as net metering credits solar producers, data metering enables ROI-driven decisions, cost allocation, and value attribution—turning data from opaque overhead into an accountable production factor. Transformation for data: from untracked "big data dumps" to granular metering (e.g., cost per query, value per dataset), enabling engineering-led investments and preventing wasteful accumulation.

- Scalability and Open Access (Plug and Play): Infrastructure features infinite scalability and frictionless entry—designed as an open platform where new loads plug in via standards. Data must provide similar open access: standardized protocols, APIs, metadata catalogs, and semantic interfaces enable new applications, AI agents, or models to "plug in" with minimal reconfiguration. This demands commitment to open standards over proprietary silos, ensuring application-layer data achieves true plug-and-play compatibility across the enterprise. The shift: data evolves from closed, vendor-locked silos (requiring custom integrations) to an elastic, open grid that scales horizontally and supports dynamic workloads without proportional engineering effort.

- Universal Data-Centric Representation ("Everything is Data"): The most transformative feature is self-referential transparency: treating all control logic, governance rules, orchestration state, and operational metadata as data itself. This makes the infrastructure inherently transparent, composable, and automatable. The key question: What should become data? Within infrastructure control and observability domains, non-data behaviors (e.g., transformation scripts, policy enforcement, failure events) must be systematically represented as structured, queryable data. This enables AI to fully orchestrate, introspect, and optimize the grid—realizing a true Data System of Systems (SoS) where components interact via rich, semantic metadata rather than brittle code. For data's change: from opaque, code-heavy configurations to a fully datafied layer, unlocking AI-driven self-optimization and 360-degree visibility.

Only when these first-principles requirements are engineered into a mature Soft Infrastructure can we guarantee a continuous, high-quality "data food supply" for current and future AI workloads. By extracting and reinterpreting time-tested methodologies from mature engineering disciplines—electrical (resilience), civil (structural integrity), industrial (process decoupling), systems (observability)—we adapt them to modern distributed environments. This cross-disciplinary foundation is a cornerstone of the book: it creates a platform so robust and invisible that it seamlessly powers the AI revolution without constant human intervention.

The urgency of this shift is driven by the Scarcity Paradox: as high-quality, human-generated data becomes increasingly scarce, traditional "data mining"—manual, artisanal sifting through digital rubble—is no longer sustainable. To fuel the AI era, we must transition to an automated Data Refinery model. The core purpose of Soft Infrastructure is to industrialize data preparation: systematically transforming raw, heterogeneous streams into high-quality, infrastructure-grade assets ready for intelligence workloads. Just as the Second Industrial Revolution required oil refineries to power combustion engines, the current era demands Soft Infrastructure to power the engines of modern intelligence.

2.3 Relationship to Existing Architecture Paradigms

This book does not propose yet another data architecture paradigm, nor does it attempt to sit "on top of" existing ones as an additional layer above data warehouses, databases, data lakes, lakehouses, or any other storage/compute system. It is not competing with or replacing established approaches such as Data Mesh, Data Fabric, Lakehouse architectures, Data Contracts, Data Observability platforms, or any particular technology stack or vendor solution.

Instead, the work operates at a fundamentally different conceptual level: the infrastructure engineering level. It starts from the paradigm shift of treating data as soft infrastructure—a continuously operating, utility-like system—and then applies first-principles thinking drawn primarily from mature disciplines such as systems engineering, industrial engineering, control engineering, and reliability engineering.

The central contribution of this book is therefore methodological, not technological:

- It focuses on methodology migration—systematically transferring proven, time-tested engineering principles, operational patterns, and design invariants from these established fields into the domain of distributed, software-defined data systems.
- Concepts presented throughout the book—such as the layered model, semantic elevation, infrastructure digital twin, trust boundaries for AI integration, deterministic system state representation, autonomous reliability enforcement, and bounded probabilistic augmentation—are not specific technologies, platforms, or implementations. They are methodological lenses and reusable engineering patterns that can (and should) be applied across any underlying architecture, storage engine, orchestration tool, governance framework, or cloud provider.

This methodological emphasis aligns directly with the very nature of true infrastructure construction. No serious infrastructure (power grids, railway networks, telecommunications backbones) has ever been built by mandating a single, rigid implementation framework or technology stack—that would be impractical, brittle, and contrary to fundamental engineering principles. Successful infrastructures succeed by establishing invariant engineering principles, standardized interfaces, and transferable patterns that allow diverse technologies, vendors, generations, and local adaptations to coexist, evolve, and interoperate reliably over decades.

The same logic applies here. The Sovereign Intelligence Grid framework is not "another data thing" to install, adopt, or migrate to. It is a higher-order engineering perspective that enables practitioners to:

- Evaluate existing architectures (Data Mesh, Lakehouse, Data Fabric, etc.) against true infrastructure-grade criteria (long-term continuity, deterministic state representation, autonomous reliability enforcement).
- Identify systemic gaps in observability, auditability, self-healing capability, and boundary control.
- Systematically migrate proven patterns from mature engineering disciplines to close those gaps.
- Achieve infrastructure maturity—reliability, predictability, and resilience at utility scale—regardless of the underlying technology choices or organizational models.

In short, this book is about how to think about data as infrastructure—not what specific tool to buy, platform to deploy, or layer to add. It provides a cross-disciplinary methodological foundation that can elevate any modern data architecture toward genuine, long-term infrastructure-grade maturity, in service of sustainable, trustworthy enterprise intelligence.

2.4 Further Reading

The arguments developed in this chapter are not speculative or metaphorical. They are grounded in established engineering disciplines that have governed the design of reliable infrastructures for over a century. Readers seeking deeper theoretical foundations for the infrastructural reclassification of data may consult the following works. Each contributes a critical dimension to understanding data as a Soft Infrastructure governed by first principles rather than tool selection.

- Rinaldi, S. M., Peerenboom, J. P., & Kelly, T. K. (2001). Identifying, understanding, and analyzing critical infrastructure interdependencies. IEEE Control Systems Magazine, 21(6), 11–25.

  - Annotation: Establishes a systems-engineering framework for analyzing cascading failures and interdependencies in critical infrastructures. Directly relevant to the chapter's argument that data failures must be bounded and isolated rather than eliminated, and that observability is prerequisite to systemic resilience.

- Maier, M. W. (1998). Architecting principles for systems-of-systems. Systems Engineering, 1(4), 267–284.

- Annotation: Defines the architectural properties of large-scale Systems-of-Systems (SoS), including operational independence and evolutionary development. Provides foundational support for conceptualizing data infrastructure as a distributed Soft Infrastructure grid composed of semi-autonomous subsystems.

- Laprie, J.-C. (1995). Dependable computing and fault tolerance: Concepts and terminology. IEEE Transactions on Dependable and Secure Computing.

  - Annotation: Formalizes the distinction between fault, error, and failure, and defines reliability as a measurable engineering attribute. Reinforces the chapter's emphasis on deterministic control, containment boundaries, and infrastructure-grade dependability in data systems.

- Wang, R. Y., & Strong, D. M. (1996). Beyond accuracy: What data quality means to data consumers. Journal of Management Information Systems, 12(4), 5–33.

  - Annotation: Introduces a multidimensional framework for evaluating data quality from the consumer perspective. Supports the Scarcity Paradox discussion by clarifying that AI-era constraints stem from governance, structure, and semantic integrity—not raw volume.

- Kaplan, J., et al. (2020). Scaling laws for neural language models. arXiv:2001.08361.

  - Annotation: Demonstrates empirically that model performance scales predictably with compute, model size, and dataset size. Reinforces the structural pressure on high-quality data supply and the need for industrialized data refinement rather than artisanal data mining.

- Armbrust, M., et al. (2010). A view of cloud computing. Communications of the ACM, 53(4), 50–58.

  - Annotation: Provides an architectural framing of elasticity, abstraction, and service-oriented infrastructure in cloud environments. Relevant to understanding Soft Infrastructure as a continuously operating, utility-like substrate.

- Åström, K. J., & Murray, R. M. (2008). Feedback Systems: An Introduction for Scientists and Engineers. Princeton University Press.

  - Annotation: Introduces foundational feedback control theory, including stability, bounded uncertainty, and controllability. Supports the chapter's central thesis that uncertainty must be confined within measurable and enforceable engineering boundaries.

Taken together, these works illustrate a consistent principle: infrastructure maturity is not achieved through the proliferation of tools or architectural fashions, but through invariant engineering properties—standardization, observability, fault containment, decoupling, and measurable control. The transition from data exhaust to data infrastructure is therefore best understood not as a technological shift, but as an engineering reclassification. By grounding data systems in the same first-principles rigor that governs power grids, transportation systems, and communication networks, we establish the conditions necessary for sustainable, trustworthy intelligence at scale.

Chapter 3
The Components of Soft Data Infrastructure

Abstract This chapter analyzes the functional components of data infrastructure, including ingestion, modeling, consumption, quality, governance and lineage, and security. Each component is evaluated through an engineering lens, emphasizing architectural structure, operational maturity, and common failure patterns. The chapter demonstrates that fragmentation across these components often results from missing lifecycle boundaries and insufficient observability. Rather than treating deficiencies as tooling limitations, it identifies structural causes that prevent systems from achieving infrastructure-grade stability. The analysis establishes the need for coordinated refinement, governance, and transmission mechanisms, laying the groundwork for the cross-disciplinary architectural blueprint introduced in the following chapter.

Keyword Data lifecycle boundaries · Infrastructure-grade stability · Data Ingestion · Data Modeling · Operational maturity · Structural observability

The transition from a resource-centric view of data to an infrastructure-led paradigm necessitates moving beyond abstract conceptual framing toward concrete engineering implementation and operational architecture. Infrastructure, by definition, is not an idea but a coordinated system of interoperable components governed by enforceable design principles. Historically, large-scale industrial transformations—such as the evolution from isolated power generators to nationally synchronized electrical grids during the Second Industrial Revolution—were enabled not by conceptual vision alone, but by the systematic integration of specialized components, including generation units, transmission mechanisms, voltage regulation systems, and distribution networks.

Similarly, the realization of a Data Soft Infrastructure in the AI era depends on the disciplined coordination of distinct engineering building blocks operating within defined boundaries. While the previous chapter established the philosophical and methodological rationale for treating data as infrastructure, the present chapter shifts focus to its structural composition and operational mechanics. We begin at the infrastructural boundary with Data Ingestion, the interface layer through which

Z. T. Lee, *The Data Grid*, SpringerBriefs in Computer Science,
https://doi.org/10.1007/978-3-032-25004-9_3

heterogeneous operational systems expose raw signals to the broader data environment. These signals originate from diverse sources—APIs, transactional databases, event streams, sensors, and external services—and must be captured with fidelity and minimal distortion. Once ingested, raw data requires structural stabilization and semantic normalization. This function is fulfilled by Data Modeling, which progressively refines information through layered transformations. In infrastructural terms, modeling performs a role analogous to voltage elevation and transmission stabilization: it enhances semantic clarity, enforces structural consistency, and prepares data for reliable long-distance propagation across analytical and intelligent workloads.

Throughout this lifecycle, Data Quality and Data Security act as systemic control and protection mechanisms. Rather than serving as isolated checkpoints, they function as continuous enforcement layers—detecting anomalies, constraining variability, preventing corruption propagation, and maintaining defined trust boundaries. These mechanisms ensure that uncertainty remains measurable and bounded rather than systemic. Finally, data reaches the Application and Self-Service Layer, where refined, semantically coherent assets are exposed through standardized interfaces for human and machine consumption. At this stage, high-fidelity signals are translated into operational metrics, analytical outputs, and AI-ready representations. The objective is not simplification for its own sake, but controlled abstraction: enabling consumption without compromising traceability, semantic integrity, or governance constraints.

Viewed through this infrastructural lens, modern data engineering is not a collection of tools or pipelines, but a coordinated refinement and transmission system. Raw, heterogeneous inputs are progressively stabilized, governed, and structured into reliable intelligence signals capable of supporting AI-driven decision systems and automated operational loops.

3.1   Data Ingestion

Data Ingestion constitutes the foundational boundary layer of a data infrastructure. It is the controlled interface through which operational production systems expose data to analytical, reporting, and AI-driven environments. In formal terms, ingestion is the systematic acquisition, transport, and registration of data from heterogeneous source systems into a governed storage substrate—such as a data warehouse, data lake, lakehouse, or object-based storage system—under defined reliability, integrity, and latency constraints. As the most upstream stage of the data lifecycle, ingestion performs three core functions:

- Acquisition—extracting data from operational or external systems without disrupting their primary workloads.
- Transport—delivering data across network and system boundaries in a fault-tolerant manner.

- Registration—ensuring that ingested data is durably stored, identifiable, and traceable within the broader infrastructure.

The objective is not merely movement of bytes, but preservation of structural integrity, temporal correctness, and semantic traceability from origin to landing zone.

3.1.1 Scope and Architectural Forms

Enterprise data ingestion must accommodate a wide spectrum of sources, including:

- Transactional databases (relational and NoSQL)
- Service APIs (REST, GraphQL)
- Event streams and messaging systems
- Log files and telemetry
- IoT and edge devices
- Third-party SaaS exports
- Batch file transfers

These sources differ significantly in update frequency, schema volatility, reliability guarantees, and access constraints. Consequently, ingestion architecture must be adaptable yet governed.

3.1.2 Mainstream Enterprise Patterns

In practice, enterprise ingestion has converged around several dominant operational patterns:

- Batch Ingestion: Scheduled extraction and load processes remain common for non-real-time workloads. Batch pipelines are typically orchestrated through workflow engines and ELT frameworks. They offer simplicity and cost efficiency but introduce latency windows.
- Streaming / Real-Time Ingestion: Event-driven ingestion supports low-latency use cases such as monitoring, fraud detection, and recommendation systems. Streaming architectures rely on durable message logs and distributed processing frameworks. They reduce latency but increase operational complexity.
- Change Data Capture (CDC): CDC mechanisms capture incremental database changes rather than performing full refreshes. This approach improves efficiency and reduces load on source systems while preserving transactional ordering semantics.
- Layered Landing (e.g., Raw/Bronze Zones): Many organizations land ingested data first in a high-fidelity raw zone before downstream transformation. This preserves an immutable source-of-record representation and supports auditability and replay.

These patterns are not mutually exclusive; mature infrastructures typically employ a hybrid combination depending on workload characteristics.

3.1.3 Common Failure Modes in Enterprise Practice

Despite tooling maturity, ingestion remains one of the most fragile layers in enterprise data systems. Recurring structural challenges include:

- Heterogeneity and Schema Volatility: Source systems evolve independently. Field additions, type changes, or API modifications can silently break pipelines or introduce semantic drift. Without explicit schema governance, ingestion becomes brittle.
- Latency Pressure vs. Correctness Guarantees: Real-time expectations conflict with exactly-once semantics, ordering guarantees, and backpressure management. Engineering trade-offs between freshness and correctness are often poorly articulated.
- Upstream Data Integrity Issues: Incomplete records, duplication, inconsistent identifiers, and malformed payloads frequently enter at ingestion. When not bounded early, such defects propagate downstream and amplify in analytical and AI workloads.
- Scalability Constraints: Large-scale telemetry, clickstreams, and AI training datasets impose high throughput requirements. Legacy ingestion mechanisms often struggle with horizontal scalability or cost efficiency at scale.
- Reliability and Recovery Complexity: Network interruptions, partial failures, retry loops, and replay handling introduce risks of duplication or data loss. Idempotency, watermarking, and checkpointing mechanisms are frequently under-engineered.
- Operational Fragmentation: Organizations commonly accumulate multiple ingestion tools across teams. This fragmentation leads to inconsistent monitoring, duplicated connectors, and weak governance visibility.
- Security and Compliance Exposure: Sensitive data may traverse external networks or cross trust boundaries during ingestion. Encryption, access control, and audit logging are sometimes retrofitted rather than designed in.

3.1.4 Why Ingestion Rarely Achieves Infrastructure-Grade Maturity

For ingestion to function as true infrastructure rather than as a collection of pipelines, several conditions must be satisfied:

- Deterministic recoverability—the ability to replay, reconcile, and reproduce ingestion state.

- Schema governance at the boundary—explicit contracts governing structural evolution.
- Observable operational state—real-time monitoring of throughput, freshness, failure rates, and drift.
- Isolation of failure domains—preventing upstream instability from cascading across workloads.
- Security-by-design controls—encryption, classification, and policy enforcement embedded at ingestion time.

In many enterprises, ingestion remains reactive rather than engineered. Pipelines are created to satisfy immediate integration needs but lack formal boundary contracts, replay guarantees, or standardized observability. As a result, ingestion becomes a recurring source of downstream instability. In the AI era, ingestion maturity is particularly critical. Machine learning and autonomous systems depend on granular, timely, and structurally consistent inputs. Latency gaps, silent corruption, or uncontrolled schema drift can degrade model reliability and erode institutional trust. Thus, ingestion should be treated not merely as data movement, but as a boundary control system: the disciplined regulation of what enters the intelligence substrate, under explicit engineering constraints.

3.2 Data Modeling

Data Modeling constitutes the structural core of a data infrastructure. It is the disciplined process through which raw, heterogeneous data is transformed into organized, semantically coherent, and reusable representations. Whereas ingestion governs the controlled intake of data, modeling establishes the relational, structural, and semantic frameworks that render data interpretable, consistent, and operationally reliable across analytical and intelligent workloads.

In formal terms, data modeling performs three core functions:

- Structural normalization—organizing data into stable schemas, keys, and relationships that eliminate ambiguity and enforce consistency.
- Semantic formalization—defining canonical entities, metrics, and business concepts under shared definitions.
- Layered abstraction—progressively refining data into bounded stages suitable for distinct categories of consumption.

The objective is not merely transformation, but the establishment of durable structural invariants that enable long-term interpretability and reuse.

3.2.1   Scope and Architectural Forms

Enterprise data modeling must accommodate multiple abstraction layers and consumption requirements. In contemporary practice, modeling commonly operates within layered architectures that distinguish between:

- Raw or Bronze layers—preserving high-fidelity source representations with minimal transformation.
- Intermediate or Silver layers—enforcing normalization, conformance, and structural integrity across domains.
- Curated or Gold layers—structuring data for defined analytical or operational use cases, often incorporating domain logic and performance considerations.

Although terminology varies, the architectural intent remains consistent: to separate preservation, normalization, and semantic exposure into clearly bounded stages with defined responsibilities. Beyond layered refinement, several structural paradigms are widely adopted:

- Dimensional modeling—organizing data into fact and dimension structures to support analytical querying.
- Data Vault and related hub-link models—emphasizing auditability, historical traceability, and adaptability under schema evolution.
- Semantic abstraction layers—decoupling business metric definitions from physical storage implementations.
- Graph-based and entity-resolution models—representing complex relationships and identity consolidation across systems.

These paradigms differ in form, but share a common objective: imposing structural coherence and shared meaning across fragmented data sources.

3.2.2   Mainstream Enterprise Patterns

In practice, enterprise modeling has converged around several recurring operational patterns. These patterns differ by organizational context and workload mix, but they reflect stable tendencies in how enterprises maintain semantic consistency at scale:

- Layered refinement workflows: Modeling is organized as a progression of bounded layers, where each layer has a distinct responsibility—preservation (raw fidelity), normalization (structural conformance), and semantic exposure (domain-ready models). This pattern supports separation of concerns and reduces coupling between upstream volatility and downstream consumers.
- Domain-oriented canonical entities: Mature environments define canonical entities (e.g., customer, account, product) within explicit domain boundaries. These entities serve as stable reference points for downstream metrics and feature definitions, reducing duplication and ambiguity.

- Metric standardization via semantic definitions: Enterprises increasingly formalize metric definitions independently of specific dashboards or storage tables. This pattern enables consistent interpretation of KPIs across tools and teams, and reduces "metric drift" over time.
- Incremental and reproducible transformations: Modeling transformations are commonly implemented as deterministic, versioned steps that can be rebuilt from source states. This supports repeatability, auditability, and controlled evolution under change.
- Dual-purpose modeling for humans and machines: Many organizations now attempt to design models that serve both traditional analytics (human interpretation) and intelligent workloads (machine consumption). This often results in parallel representations—human-facing aggregates and machine-facing granular, time-indexed structures—linked through shared entity foundations.

These patterns do not mandate a particular technology stack. They describe operational regularities that appear whenever modeling is treated as a long-lived structural discipline rather than as report-specific data shaping.

3.2.3 Common Failure Modes in Enterprise Practice

Despite methodological maturity, modeling frequently becomes one of the most structurally fragile layers within enterprise data systems. Recurring challenges include:

- Semantic inconsistency—identical business concepts may be defined differently across teams or domains. Without centralized governance, metrics diverge across reports and pipelines, undermining trust.
- Premature aggregation and loss of granularity—optimization for reporting performance often eliminates event-level detail required for longitudinal analysis, AI feature engineering, or reproducibility. Lost fidelity cannot be reconstructed.
- Model proliferation and dependency complexity—incremental additions of tables and transformations without clear ownership create dense dependency networks. Minor upstream changes may cascade unpredictably.
- Manual bottlenecks—heavy reliance on handcrafted SQL transformations slows iteration and encourages parallel, ungoverned modeling paths.
- Governance and ownership gaps—unclear stewardship leads to duplicated entities, overlapping definitions, and inconsistent abstractions.
- AI-readiness misalignment—models optimized for dashboard consumption may lack the granularity, temporal continuity, or entity resolution required by machine-driven workloads.

These weaknesses are structural rather than technological; they arise from insufficient invariants rather than insufficient tools.

3.2.4   Why Modeling Rarely Achieves Infrastructure-Grade Maturity

For modeling to function as a true infrastructural discipline rather than as an evolving collection of transformations, several conditions must be satisfied:

- Stable semantic contracts—canonical entity and metric definitions must be explicitly governed and consistently reused.
- Preservation of recoverable fidelity—refinement must not eliminate access to high-resolution source states required for future analysis.
- Clear boundary separation—normalization, enrichment, and consumption logic must remain structurally distinct.
- Explicit ownership and stewardship—modeling responsibilities must be defined at domain level.
- Deterministic lineage and traceability—transformation paths must be reproducible and auditable across layers.

In many enterprises, modeling evolves reactively. Structures are introduced to satisfy immediate reporting needs without long-term invariants. Over time, accumulated inconsistencies resemble architectural debt rather than engineered design. When semantic coherence degrades, downstream systems inherit instability. Metrics diverge, analytical outputs conflict, and AI pipelines require independent reconstruction of features. Trust becomes conditional rather than structural. Accordingly, modeling must be treated not as a reporting convenience, but as a foundational structural discipline governed by explicit design principles.

3.3   Data Consumption

Data Consumption constitutes the controlled exposure layer of a data infrastructure. It is the stage at which structured and modeled data assets are made available for interpretation, automation, and decision execution. Whereas ingestion governs intake and modeling governs structural refinement, consumption governs standardized access. Its function is not to reshape data, but to present it through stable, governed interfaces suitable for human and machine interaction. In formal terms, data consumption performs three core functions:

- Exposure—providing structured access points to curated entities, metrics, and features.
- Standardization—ensuring consistent interpretation of business logic across tools and systems.
- Operationalization—enabling analytical insight, automation workflows, and AI inference to act upon structured data.

The objective is not visualization alone, but the reliable translation of engineered data structures into actionable intelligence.

3.3.1 Scope and Architectural Forms

Enterprise consumption must support multiple audiences, latency requirements, and execution contexts. In contemporary architectures, consumption commonly manifests through several structural forms:

- Business Intelligence interfaces—human-facing environments where curated data models are queried, visualized, and interpreted.
- Semantic abstraction layers—logical definitions of metrics and entities decoupled from physical storage, enabling consistency across diverse consumption channels.
- Programmatic interfaces—APIs and service endpoints through which applications and workflows retrieve structured data directly.
- Embedded and operational integration—structured data integrated into transactional systems, digital products, or automated processes.
- AI-driven interfaces—systems that consume structured data as features or context for inference, recommendation, or autonomous decision-making.

Although these forms differ in interface design and latency sensitivity, they share a common dependency: structural coherence and semantic determinism established upstream.

3.3.2 Mainstream Enterprise Patterns

In practice, enterprise consumption converges around several recurring operational patterns:

- Dashboard-centric exposure: Curated datasets are optimized for interactive reporting and KPI tracking. Consumption logic is frequently embedded within visualization tools.
- Centralized semantic definitions: Organizations increasingly define metrics and entities in shared logical layers to reduce cross-tool inconsistency.
- Programmatic feature serving: Structured data is exposed through APIs or feature stores for application and AI use.
- Dual-channel access: Separate representations are maintained for human-readable aggregates and machine-consumable granular data, often linked through shared entity identifiers.
- Access-governed endpoints: Consumption interfaces are wrapped with role-based or attribute-based access policies to regulate exposure.

These patterns reflect attempts to standardize exposure without constraining flexibility. However, they vary widely in rigor and consistency across organizations.

3.3.3 Common Failure Modes in Enterprise Practice

Despite tooling maturity, the consumption layer often reveals systemic weaknesses. Recurring structural challenges include:

- Metric inconsistency—divergent business logic across dashboards and tools leads to conflicting outputs and erosion of trust.
- Human-centric optimization—models designed primarily for reporting may not support machine-driven workloads, creating parallel infrastructures.
- Performance-fidelity tension—aggregated structures improve reporting responsiveness but may sacrifice detail required for analytical depth or AI training.
- Traceability gaps—exposed metrics or features may lack transparent lineage back to source transformations, complicating auditability.
- Cost amplification—high-concurrency querying and real-time inference workloads increase computational expenditure when exposure is not governed.
- Shadow consumption paths—teams bypass official interfaces when perceived latency or rigidity obstructs operational needs, weakening systemic coherence.

These weaknesses typically reflect upstream structural instability rather than interface design alone.

3.3.4 Why Consumption Rarely Achieves Infrastructure-Grade Maturity

For consumption to function as a true infrastructural exposure layer rather than as a collection of reporting surfaces, several conditions must be satisfied:

- Semantic determinism—business definitions must be declared once and reused consistently across all interfaces.
- Standardized access contracts—exposure endpoints must be stable, documented, and versioned.
- Deterministic lineage—every exposed metric, feature, or signal must be traceable to source transformations.
- Latency-aligned architecture—consumption modes must be matched explicitly to workload requirements without compromising data fidelity.
- Integrated access governance—exposure must respect defined security and compliance boundaries.
- Machine-readiness—interfaces must support both interpretive (human) and operational (machine) consumption.

In many enterprises, consumption evolves reactively. Dashboards and APIs are introduced to satisfy immediate needs without shared invariants. Over time, fragmentation accumulates: metrics diverge, AI pipelines reconstruct logic independently, and cost grows unpredictably. When engineered under explicit structural principles, consumption becomes a standardized exposure interface through which intelligence—human or artificial—interacts with a governed substrate. When left unstructured, it magnifies inconsistency. Accordingly, consumption must be treated not as a visualization endpoint, but as a formalized interface discipline within the infrastructure.

3.4 Data Quality

Data Quality constitutes the regulatory control layer of a data infrastructure. It is the disciplined process through which data integrity, consistency, and fitness-for-purpose are continuously specified, validated, and enforced across the lifecycle. Whereas ingestion governs boundary intake, modeling governs structural coherence, and consumption governs exposure, quality governs admissibility and stability. Its function is not transformation, but constraint. In formal terms, data quality performs three core functions:

- Validation—verifying that data conforms to structural, statistical, and semantic constraints.
- Monitoring—observing freshness, distributional stability, and behavioral drift over time.
- Enforcement—preventing the propagation of defective data through quarantine, rejection, alerting, or rollback mechanisms.

The objective is not the elimination of all anomalies, but the containment of variability within defined and measurable tolerances.

3.4.1 Scope and Architectural Forms

Data quality operates across all architectural layers, with responsibilities that vary by abstraction level. At ingestion boundaries, quality emphasizes structural validity, completeness, schema conformity, and temporal correctness. At modeling layers, it focuses on referential integrity, normalization consistency, and cross-domain conformance. At curated and consumption layers, it extends to business-rule validation, semantic coherence, and metric reliability. Quality therefore cannot be implemented as a single checkpoint. It must be distributed and layer-aware, with explicit validation scopes aligned to architectural boundaries. Architecturally, quality mechanisms typically appear in three structural forms:

- Embedded validation within transformation workflows.
- Independent monitoring systems observing datasets and metadata.
- Boundary-level contracts specifying admissibility conditions between producers and consumers.

These forms differ in placement but share a common purpose: to regulate propagation across structural layers.

3.4.2 Mainstream Enterprise Patterns

In practice, enterprise quality control converges around several recurring operational patterns:

- Rule-based validation frameworks: Declarative constraints enforce non-null requirements, uniqueness, referential integrity, acceptable value ranges, and freshness thresholds.
- Continuous observability: Monitoring systems track distributional anomalies, volume shifts, latency deviations, and schema changes, linking incidents to lineage metadata.
- Contract-based enforcement: Explicit agreements define schema invariants, timeliness expectations, and service-level conditions at domain boundaries.
- Statistical drift detection: Distribution-aware mechanisms identify gradual deviations not captured by static rules.
- Layered validation models: Different validation intensities are applied at raw, normalized, and curated stages to balance fidelity preservation and semantic correctness.

These patterns represent attempts to formalize control. However, their effectiveness depends on governance discipline rather than tool availability.

3.4.3 Common Failure Modes in Enterprise Practice

Despite increased automation, data quality frequently remains reactive. Recurring structural challenges include:

- Undetected drift—schema evolution, identifier reinterpretation, or statistical distribution shifts may occur gradually without triggering explicit alarms.
- Rule proliferation—expanding datasets generate increasing numbers of validation rules, often without clear ownership or lifecycle management.
- Alert fatigue—poorly calibrated thresholds produce excessive notifications, reducing operational responsiveness.
- Latency trade-offs—real-time validation introduces computational overhead, leading teams to relax enforcement under performance pressure.

- Business-logic ambiguity—cross-system semantic constraints are difficult to encode consistently, especially when domain ownership is fragmented.
- AI amplification effects—minor structural inconsistencies may propagate into model features, degrading reproducibility and interpretability without immediate visibility.

These weaknesses arise not from lack of checking mechanisms, but from insufficient integration of quality into structural design principles.

3.4.4 Why Data Quality Rarely Achieves Infrastructure-Grade Maturity

For quality to function as a true infrastructural control system rather than as episodic inspection, several conditions must be satisfied:

- Quality-as-code—validation logic must be version-controlled, testable, and reproducible alongside transformation logic.
- Layer-bound enforcement—validation responsibilities must be explicitly assigned to architectural stages.
- Deterministic remediation—defined procedures must exist for isolation, replay, reconciliation, and rollback.
- Observable state representation—measurable indicators of freshness, anomaly rates, and violation patterns must be continuously available.
- Failure containment—defective data must be isolated to prevent cross-domain propagation.
- Explicit stewardship—accountability for rule definition and maintenance must be assigned at domain level.

In many enterprises, quality controls are introduced after incidents rather than embedded by design. As a result, enforcement becomes patchwork rather than systemic. When embedded into architectural boundaries and governed through deterministic controls, quality stabilizes the entire infrastructure. When treated as optional validation, it becomes a recurring source of downstream instability. Accordingly, Data Quality must be treated not as inspection, but as a formal control discipline governing the admissibility and propagation of data across the intelligence substrate.

3.5 Data Governance and Lineage

Data Governance and Lineage constitute the control-plane layer of a data infrastructure. They define the rules under which data is classified, accessed, modified, and audited, and they provide the traceable representation of how data moves and transforms across the system. Whereas ingestion governs intake, modeling governs structure, consumption governs exposure, and quality governs admissibility, governance governs authority and accountability. In formal terms, this layer performs three core functions:

- Policy definition—specifying classification standards, access rules, retention policies, and compliance constraints.
- Stewardship and accountability—assigning ownership, responsibility, and review processes at dataset and domain levels.
- Traceable lineage representation—capturing and exposing the full transformation history of data from source through downstream derivations.

The objective is not documentation alone, but enforceable transparency and operational accountability across the lifecycle.

3.5.1   Scope and Architectural Forms

Governance and lineage operate across all structural layers and organizational domains. Their scope includes:

- Data classification—defining sensitivity levels, regulatory categories, and domain ownership.
- Access control—regulating who may view, modify, or export specific datasets or attributes.
- Lifecycle management—governing retention, archival, deletion, and versioning policies.
- Auditability and compliance—ensuring that data transformations and exposures can be reconstructed and verified.

Architecturally, governance typically manifests in three structural forms:

- Centralized metadata catalogs—maintaining inventory, ownership, and classification information.
- Policy enforcement mechanisms—embedding access controls and rule evaluation at query or pipeline boundaries.
- Automated lineage capture—recording transformation paths, dependencies, and execution context across ingestion, modeling, and consumption layers.

Although these components may be implemented through different tools or platforms, their function is systemic: to make the infrastructure observable, controllable, and accountable.

3.5.2 *Mainstream Enterprise Patterns*

Enterprise governance and lineage practices commonly converge around several operational patterns:

- Centralized metadata repositories—organizations maintain unified catalogs that register datasets, schemas, owners, and classifications to reduce fragmentation.
- Runtime lineage capture—transformation frameworks emit metadata describing data movement and dependency relationships, enabling forward and backward traceability.
- Policy-as-code enforcement—access rules and classification policies are defined declaratively and enforced programmatically at execution time.
- Domain-aligned stewardship—data ownership responsibilities are assigned at business-domain level rather than purely technical boundaries.
- Automated classification assistance—metadata enrichment and tagging processes support scalability under growing data volumes.

These patterns aim to move governance from static documentation toward operational enforcement. However, maturity varies significantly across enterprises.

3.5.3 *Common Failure Modes in Enterprise Practice*

Despite increased attention to governance, structural weaknesses persist:

- Lineage gaps—incomplete instrumentation or opaque transformations create "dark zones" where transformation paths cannot be reconstructed.
- Governance fragmentation—multiple catalogs and policy systems coexist without synchronization, producing inconsistent enforcement.
- Stale metadata—ownership and classification information may not be updated as systems evolve, weakening accountability.
- Compliance retrofitting—regulatory requirements are often addressed reactively, leading to ad hoc audit mechanisms rather than embedded controls.
- Scalability pressure—as data volume and transformation complexity increase, lineage metadata itself becomes large and costly to maintain.
- AI explainability deficits—without granular lineage and transformation transparency, AI-derived outputs may lack reconstructible derivation paths, especially in regulated environments.

These weaknesses do not arise from conceptual ambiguity, but from insufficient integration of governance into architectural design.

3.5.4 Why Governance and Lineage Rarely Achieve Infrastructure-Grade Maturity

For governance and lineage to function as a true infrastructural control plane rather than as documentation overlays, several conditions must be satisfied:

- Comprehensive lineage capture—transformation events must be systematically recorded across ingestion, modeling, and consumption layers.
- Deterministic reproducibility—lineage must enable reconstruction of dataset state at defined points in time.
- Integrated policy enforcement—access and classification rules must be embedded in execution paths rather than applied externally.
- Domain-level accountability—ownership and stewardship must be explicitly assigned and reviewable.
- Tamper-evident audit trails—historical transformation and access records must be preserved under defined retention controls.

In many enterprises, governance is implemented as a cataloging initiative rather than as an enforcement system. Lineage may be partially captured but not continuously validated. As a result, transparency becomes approximate rather than deterministic. When engineered as a structural control plane, governance and lineage provide the conditions for auditability, reproducibility, and institutional trust. When treated as metadata decoration, they create an illusion of control without operational authority. Accordingly, governance and lineage must be treated not as administrative overlays, but as enforceable structural mechanisms that define and preserve accountability within the intelligence substrate.

3.6 Data Security

Data Security constitutes the containment and protection layer of a data infrastructure. It defines and enforces the mechanisms through which data assets are safeguarded against unauthorized access, corruption, leakage, and malicious manipulation. Whereas governance establishes authority and accountability, security enforces boundary protection at technical and operational levels. In formal terms, data security performs three core functions:

- Access control—regulating who may read, modify, transmit, or execute operations on data assets.
- Cryptographic protection—ensuring confidentiality and integrity during storage, transmission, and processing.
- Threat detection and containment—identifying and isolating malicious activity, misuse, or anomalous behavior.

The objective is not merely prevention, but the preservation of structural trust boundaries within the intelligence substrate.

3.6.1 Scope and Architectural Forms

Security must operate across all layers of the infrastructure and across organizational boundaries. Its scope includes:

- Identity and authentication—verifying the identity of users, services, and automated agents.
- Authorization and access governance—enforcing role-based and attribute-based access constraints.
- Encryption controls—protecting data at rest, in transit, and during computation.
- Data masking and anonymization—reducing exposure of sensitive attributes in downstream contexts.
- Monitoring and intrusion detection—identifying unauthorized access, data exfiltration, or manipulation attempts.

Security mechanisms typically manifest in three architectural forms:

- Embedded enforcement within storage and query engines.
- Network-level and perimeter controls regulating data movement.
- Runtime monitoring systems analyzing access patterns and anomaly behavior.

These forms collectively define the containment perimeter of the infrastructure.

3.6.2 Mainstream Enterprise Patterns

Enterprise security practices commonly converge around several operational patterns:

- Zero-trust access models—assuming no implicit trust between services or users, requiring continuous authentication and authorization validation.
- Fine-grained access enforcement—applying row-level, column-level, or attribute-level restrictions rather than coarse dataset-level permissions.
- Encryption-by-default policies—enforcing cryptographic protection across storage and transport layers.
- Policy-as-code security controls—declaratively defining authorization rules that are programmatically evaluated during execution.
- Integrated monitoring and response—coupling access logging with automated detection of anomalous behavior.
- AI-aware protections—extending security controls to feature stores, inference endpoints, and training datasets.

These patterns represent attempts to embed protection within the operational fabric rather than relying solely on perimeter defenses.

3.6.3 Common Failure Modes in Enterprise Practice

Despite mature security frameworks, structural weaknesses persist:

- Privilege overextension—excessive or poorly scoped permissions increase exposure risk.
- Configuration drift—inconsistent enforcement across environments creates unintended vulnerabilities.
- Fragmented policy enforcement—disparate systems implement access rules independently, producing uneven security boundaries.
- Shadow data replication—unmanaged copies of datasets proliferate across tools and environments, bypassing central controls.
- Supply-chain exposure—external data sources or third-party integrations introduce risks beyond direct organizational oversight.
- AI-specific vulnerabilities—adversarial inputs, model inversion risks, and feature poisoning introduce attack surfaces not present in traditional BI environments.
- Performance-security trade-offs—strong encryption and fine-grained checks may introduce latency, leading teams to weaken enforcement under operational pressure.

These weaknesses often arise from misalignment between security intent and architectural integration.

3.6.4 Why Security Rarely Achieves Infrastructure-Grade Maturity

For security to function as a true containment layer rather than as a reactive safeguard, several conditions must be satisfied:

- Unified identity and policy management—consistent authorization logic across all infrastructure layers.
- Deterministic enforcement—access decisions must be evaluated systematically and reproducibly.
- Comprehensive logging and traceability—every access and modification event must be auditable.
- Boundary isolation—compromise in one domain must not cascade into unrelated domains.
- Security-by-design architecture—protection controls must be embedded at ingestion, modeling, and consumption boundaries rather than added retroactively.

- Machine-context protection—AI-driven processes and automated agents must operate within the same security constraints as human actors.

In many enterprises, security is partially centralized but unevenly implemented. Controls may exist in storage layers yet be bypassed through data exports, embedded tools, or shadow workflows. As a result, enforcement becomes inconsistent. When integrated into architectural boundaries and governed under deterministic policy models, security preserves trust in the intelligence substrate. When treated as an external overlay, it becomes reactive and fragmented. Accordingly, Data Security must be treated not as perimeter defense alone, but as a structural containment discipline embedded throughout the infrastructure lifecycle.

3.7 Further Reading

The arguments developed in this chapter are grounded in formal research traditions spanning database systems, distributed computing, information quality, security engineering, and data management theory. The infrastructural treatment of ingestion, modeling, governance, quality, and security is not a stylistic reframing, but a structural alignment with decades of systems research. Readers seeking deeper theoretical foundations for the engineering discipline underlying modern data infrastructures may consult the following works.

- Gray, J., & Reuter, A. (1992). Transaction Processing: Concepts and Techniques. Morgan Kaufmann.

  - Annotation: A foundational text on atomicity, consistency, isolation, and durability (ACID) in distributed systems. Provides theoretical grounding for deterministic ingestion, recoverability, and structural correctness in storage-backed infrastructures.

- Stonebraker, M., et al. (2005). The end of an architectural era (it's time for a complete rewrite). Proceedings of VLDB.

  - Annotation: Critiques legacy database architectures and motivates system redesign under modern workloads. Relevant to modeling-layer redesign and the structural separation between preservation, normalization, and exposure layers.

- Hellerstein, J. M. (2010). The declarative imperative: Experiences and conjectures in distributed logic. SIGMOD Record, 39(1), 5–19.

  - Annotation: Explores declarative abstractions in distributed data systems. Supports the chapter's emphasis on structural invariants, deterministic transformation semantics, and reproducibility across modeling and consumption layers.

- Simmhan, Y., Plale, B., & Gannon, D. (2005). A survey of data provenance techniques. ACM SIGMOD Record, 34(3), 31–36.

  - Annotation: Provides formal treatment of data provenance and lineage models. Directly relevant to governance and traceability requirements for infrastructure-grade accountability.

- Buneman, P., Khanna, S., & Tan, W.-C. (2001). Why and where: A characterization of data provenance. Proceedings of ICDT.

  - Annotation: Establishes theoretical foundations for provenance semantics. Reinforces the need for deterministic lineage representation in distributed data systems.

- Rahm, E., & Do, H. H. (2000). Data cleaning: Problems and current approaches. IEEE Data Engineering Bulletin.

  - Annotation: A structured survey of data quality methodologies. Grounds the quality layer in formal problem categories rather than tool-centric validation practices.

- Saltzer, J. H., Reed, D. P., & Clark, D. D. (1984). End-to-end arguments in system design. ACM Transactions on Computer Systems, 2(4), 277–288.

  - Annotation: Introduces the end-to-end principle in distributed system design. Directly relevant to boundary placement, failure containment, and architectural layering across ingestion and consumption layers.

- Shapiro, M., et al. (2011). Conflict-free replicated data types. Stabilization, Safety, and Security of Distributed Systems.

  - Annotation: Formalizes convergence guarantees in distributed state systems. Supports reasoning about deterministic state representation and resilience under distributed ingestion and transformation.

- Sabelfeld, A., & Myers, A. C. (2003). Language-based information-flow security. IEEE Journal on Selected Areas in Communications, 21(1), 5–19.

  - Annotation: Provides a formal model for controlling information flow and preventing leakage. Relevant to structural containment and security-layer enforcement in intelligence infrastructures.

- Papernot, N., et al. (2016). The limitations of deep learning in adversarial settings. IEEE European Symposium on Security and Privacy.

  - Annotation: Demonstrates vulnerabilities of machine learning systems under adversarial input. Reinforces the need for structural security controls and bounded exposure in AI-driven consumption layers.

Taken together, these works illustrate a consistent principle: infrastructure maturity emerges from enforceable invariants—deterministic state management, explicit boundary control, traceable lineage, information-flow containment, and reproducible transformation semantics. The discipline of data infrastructure therefore aligns more closely with distributed systems engineering and dependable computing than with tool selection or dashboard design. The transition from fragmented data pipelines to engineered Soft Infrastructure is best understood as a shift from integration convenience to structural governance. By grounding ingestion, modeling, quality enforcement, governance, and security in first-principles systems research, we establish the conditions necessary for resilient, auditable, and scalable intelligence substrates capable of supporting AI-era workloads.

Chapter 4
Architecting the Soft Data Infrastructure—A Cross-Disciplinary Blueprint

Abstract This chapter presents the core architectural framework of the Data Grid. Drawing on principles from electrical systems, communication layering, and system-of-systems engineering, it formalizes four methodological dimensions: lifecycle segmentation, semantic elevation, declarative system representation, and bounded AI integration. Together, these dimensions define structural boundaries that isolate volatility, preserve transparency, and ensure deterministic execution. The chapter reinterprets layered architectures as infrastructure doctrine rather than implementation convention and introduces the concept of a Deterministic Structural Core. By transferring mature engineering principles into distributed software-defined environments, the chapter provides a governing blueprint for stable and scalable data infrastructure construction.

Keyword Deterministic structural core · Cross-disciplinary architecture · Lifecycle segmentation · Semantic elevation · Declarative system representation · Bounded AI integration

After outlining the functional components of data infrastructure in the previous chapter, this chapter shifts the focus from what these components are to how they are systematically integrated into a resilient and evolvable data system. It establishes the architectural and methodological foundation for the remainder of the book. Rather than introducing additional technical elements, we concentrate on the governing principles that determine structural organization, responsibility boundaries, and long-term adaptability under evolving business and technological conditions. Adopting an infrastructure-centric perspective, this chapter proposes a multidisciplinary framework for constructing modern data systems as Soft Infrastructure. Our goal is to formalize the structural logic that often remains implicit in data architecture—the mechanisms that enable scalability, reuse, and sustained evolution. By reinterpreting engineering principles from mature physical infrastructures within distributed, software-defined environments, we reposition data engineering from fragmented customization toward disciplined infrastructural practice.

Z. T. Lee, *The Data Grid*, SpringerBriefs in Computer Science, https://doi.org/10.1007/978-3-032-25004-9_4

A central conceptual shift underlies this approach. Structured data assets—most commonly tables—constitute the primary operational medium of the data infrastructure. Capabilities such as data quality enforcement, governance, security, orchestration, and observability serve as supporting subsystems whose role is to stabilize, regulate, and protect the continuity of these core assets. This mirrors mature physical infrastructures, where primary transmission networks are safeguarded by monitoring and control systems. Recognizing this primary–supporting system distinction is essential to designing resilient and evolvable data infrastructure. To structure this perspective, the chapter introduces four complementary methodological dimensions:

- Lifecycle Infrastructure Methodology. Inspired by electrical grid design, this dimension emphasizes responsibility separation across stages of generation, stabilization, transmission, and consumption. Applied to data systems, layered architectures (e.g., Bronze, Silver, Gold) are not implementation templates but structural responsibility boundaries that preserve stability while maintaining optionality and long-term evolvability.
- Semantic Processing Methodology. Drawing from layered communication protocol design, this dimension explains how semantics accumulate progressively as data flows through processing layers. Structured metadata, lineage encoding, quality signals, and domain context enrich raw data over time, transforming it into trusted, infrastructure-grade assets. Semantic layering provides the foundation for consistent transformation, traceability, and distributed interpretability.
- System Representation Methodology. This dimension advances the principle that system behavior itself should be represented as structured data. Transformation logic, orchestration states, governance rules, and execution telemetry migrate from procedural code into declarative, metadata-driven models. By datafying the infrastructure layer itself, heterogeneity is reduced and the system becomes self-descriptive, governable, and optimizable—forming the basis for recursive digital twin capabilities.
- Controlled AI-Augmented Implementation. Finally, this dimension defines how AI can be safely integrated within infrastructure boundaries. Rather than delegating control to opaque AI processes, AI is positioned as an augmentation layer operating within deterministic, version-controlled execution frameworks. Drawing on control and risk engineering principles, this approach establishes explicit boundaries between human governance and AI-assisted optimization.

Together, these four dimensions form a unified methodological foundation. The lifecycle perspective governs structural stability, the semantic perspective governs meaning accumulation, the representation perspective governs formalization and automation, and the AI boundary perspective governs safe augmentation. The chapters that follow apply these dimensions in sequence, translating abstract principles into a coherent, infrastructure-grade data system design.

4.1 The Horizontal Lifecycle View

Layered structure in infrastructure design is not an aesthetic preference; it is a structural necessity. Enduring infrastructures—electrical grids, transportation systems, and communication backbones—rely on hierarchical segmentation to regulate flow, isolate responsibility, and prevent systemic instability. Resilience is not achieved through flexibility alone; it is achieved through disciplined separation of function. When lifecycle responsibilities overlap, fragility emerges. Generation logic begins embedding consumption assumptions, stabilization mechanisms entangle with downstream intent, and local optimizations propagate global instability. Mature infrastructure engineering therefore enforces layers not as implementation convenience, but as boundary contracts that preserve long-term structural integrity.

Data infrastructure governs a flowing resource with comparable lifecycle characteristics. Data is generated, ingested, standardized, transformed, transmitted, and ultimately consumed to produce business value. Because data behaves as a lifecycle-based flow, its architecture must reflect lifecycle segmentation. Layering is not merely progressive refinement; it is responsibility allocation across stages of movement, ensuring that change in one stage does not destabilize the entire system. Without such segmentation, data architectures degrade into tightly coupled pipelines that are difficult to scale, audit, or evolve.

The widely adopted Medallion architecture—Bronze, Silver, and Gold—marked an important step toward structural order in modern data engineering. By separating raw ingestion from standardized processing and domain transformation, it introduced a practical vocabulary for staged refinement. This book does not replace that structure; it formalizes and stabilizes it by grounding it in infrastructure doctrine. Bronze, Silver, and Gold are reinterpreted not as tooling templates or maturity indicators, but as lifecycle boundary layers within a regulated flow system. The objective is not architectural novelty, but architectural clarification.

By aligning these layers with the structural logic of electrical infrastructure—generation, grid stabilization, and transmission—we move from pattern adoption to principle alignment. In electrical systems, generation facilities are structurally decoupled from transmission networks, and transmission networks are decoupled from localized consumption behavior. This separation ensures scalability, reliability, and adaptability. Applying the same reasoning clarifies why raw ingestion must remain source-faithful, why standardization must remain semantically neutral, and why domain-level modeling must preserve optionality. When layering is justified by infrastructure doctrine rather than tooling convention, its boundaries become enforceable rather than aspirational.

Within this book, the Data Grid is defined as a regulated lifecycle flow system. A grid is not merely a collection of components; it is an ordered structure governing movement through disciplined segmentation. Bronze corresponds to generation discipline, ensuring completeness and traceability. Silver corresponds to system-wide compatibility enforcement. Gold corresponds to transmission optimization, producing reusable domain-ready structures while preserving flexibility. These are not convenience stages; they are responsibility stages. Viewing layered data architecture through this lifecycle lens achieves three outcomes: it eliminates ambiguity through principled justification, defines non-negotiable boundaries that prevent semantic leakage, and embeds engineering rigor into system design. Layering is not structural complexity; it is structural order under movement. In infrastructure systems, order enables scale, resilience, and evolution. The horizontal lifecycle view establishes this order as the foundational discipline of the Data Grid.

4.1.1   Ingestion Consistency Layer

The Ingestion Consistency Layer exists to preserve an unimpeachable source baseline. In any flow-based infrastructure, the first stage is designed for fidelity, not convenience. Electrical grids begin at generation boundaries. Power plants do not optimize output for particular appliances; they inject energy reliably and traceably into the system. If this boundary is compromised, downstream stabilization loses meaning because the system no longer knows what it is regulating.

Data infrastructure faces the same requirement. Before data can be standardized or interpreted, the system must establish a reproducible entry state—a source-equivalent truth that can be replayed, audited, and reconstructed. This is the purpose of the Ingestion Consistency Layer, commonly referred to as Bronze or Raw Data. It is not casual storage; it is the generation discipline of the Data Grid and the first segment of the Deterministic Structural Core (DSC).

Without a stable ingestion baseline, the system cannot answer a fundamental engineering question: what is the reference truth when something breaks? If data is filtered, enriched, deduplicated, or reshaped at entry for convenience, neutrality is lost. When assumptions later change, the infrastructure lacks a trustworthy origin state. The consequence is not only technical debt but epistemic debt—the system can no longer prove its own history.

The absence or dilution of this layer produces three failures: auditability collapses, failure isolation becomes impossible, and long-term optionality degrades. Premature shaping restricts future reuse. Infrastructure loses its most valuable property—its ability to evolve without reconstructing itself. This requirement intensifies in AI-supported environments. AI systems can assist interpretation, but they cannot restore overwritten truth. When probabilistic inference is applied to distorted origin states, uncertainty amplifies rather than contains itself. A stable ingestion baseline is therefore not merely governance discipline; it is a prerequisite for safe AI augmentation within deterministic boundaries. The Ingestion Consistency Layer anchors the lifecycle by guaranteeing reproducible origin. Without it, subsequent layers may exist, but the system they form is no longer infrastructure in the engineering sense—it becomes a chain of transformations without a provable beginning.

4.1.2 Engineering Validity Layer

If ingestion establishes the generation boundary, the Engineering Validity Layer establishes the integration boundary. In electrical infrastructure, energy cannot enter long-distance transmission networks without stabilization. Substations normalize voltage and enforce compatibility. This stage ensures interoperability, not consumption optimization. Similarly, raw data—even faithfully preserved—is rarely immediately interoperable. Schemas differ, encodings vary, identifiers conflict. The Engineering Validity Layer (Silver) enforces structural correctness and technical compatibility across the grid. It performs normalization, deduplication, constraint validation, and schema alignment. Its mandate is compatibility, not interpretation.

This separation is structural. If business semantics enter this layer, compatibility collapses into specialization. What should function as shared infrastructure becomes domain-specific artifact. When this boundary is violated, reusability declines and stability erodes. As business definitions evolve, embedded semantics force foundational reprocessing, multiplying fragility. Like substations cannot embed appliance logic into voltage regulation, the Engineering Validity Layer must remain insulated from domain meaning. It forms the second segment of the DSC, protecting structural integrity from semantic volatility. Without it, the Data Grid fragments into partially standardized artifacts shaped by competing pressures.

4.1.3 Canonical Modeling Layer

If Silver stabilizes the grid, Gold establishes the transmission backbone. High-voltage transmission networks deliver standardized energy efficiently without determining how it will be consumed. Transmission preserves possibility. Likewise, once data is ingested faithfully and stabilized structurally, it must be organized into canonical domain entities capable of traveling across organizational boundaries without embedding application-specific assumptions. The defining principle of Gold is optionality preservation.

Gold operates at the finest meaningful grain. Early aggregation or dashboard-specific modeling compromises reuse. If canonical models embed transient application semantics, the backbone becomes rigid. What should function as shared infrastructure becomes a pre-packaged product.

If applications consume directly from Gold without adaptation layers, coupling intensifies. Minor analytical changes propagate upstream. Innovation slows. Infrastructure begins resembling a monolith rather than a grid. Gold therefore represents the final segment of the DSC. It enforces deterministic modeling discipline while preserving semantic richness for broad reuse. Transmission precedes interpretation (Fig. 4.1).

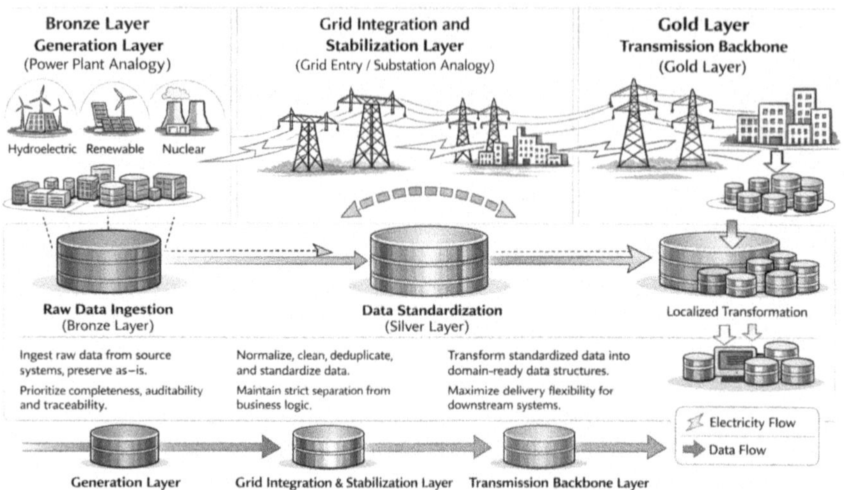

Fig. 4.1 This diagram illustrates how the data grid parallels the pre-consumption stages of an electrical grid. The Bronze Layer ingests raw data, much like power generation. The Silver Layer cleans and standardizes data, akin to grid stabilization. The Gold Layer acts as the transmission backbone, transforming data into reusable, canonical models. As electricity must flow through regulated stages before reaching consumers, data must pass through these structured layers before application-specific usage, ensuring consistency, scalability, and flexibility

4.1.4 Business Component Layer

Above the Deterministic Structural Core lies the Business Component Layer. If Gold preserves transmission integrity, this layer introduces controlled domain semantics while absorbing volatility. Business definitions evolve. KPIs shift. Regulatory rules change. Embedding such volatility within canonical models destabilizes infrastructure. The Business Component Layer isolates domain composition—aggregations, composite metrics, reusable domain views—while preserving canonical neutrality.

This layer acts as a volatility buffer. It acknowledges that meaning must be constructed, but contains it within controlled boundaries. Canonical entities remain pure; domain interpretation evolves above them. Ignoring this boundary leads to canonical pollution and systemic regression risk. Seemingly minor KPI adjustments cascade into structural modifications. Infrastructure begins inheriting business volatility. The Business Component Layer therefore enables composability without contamination. It introduces semantic flexibility while preserving deterministic foundations.

4.1.5 Application Intelligence Layer

The Application Intelligence Layer encompasses dashboards, feature tables, AI training datasets, and decision interfaces. It is the most specialized and most volatile layer. Here, variability is intentional. Applications prioritize interpretability and contextual relevance. However, variability must not flow downward. If application concerns reshape canonical structures, infrastructure fragments into product-specific forks. In AI-augmented environments, this risk intensifies. Probabilistic systems experiment and infer. If such behavior modifies structural layers within the DSC, uncertainty propagates beyond containment.

The architecture therefore enforces a Determinism Gradient. Determinism is strongest at the bottom (Bronze, Silver, Gold), relaxes through the Business Component Layer, and becomes most flexible at the Application Intelligence Layer. This gradient permits innovation while preserving structural invariants. When the gradient collapses, brittleness emerges. Error propagation radius expands. Auditability declines. What should function as a regulated grid devolves into entanglement. Controlled specialization is therefore permitted only above protected structural cores.

4.1.6 Lifecycle Segmentation as Infrastructure Doctrine

The five-layer lifecycle architecture is not an arbitrary expansion of Medallion patterns. It is grounded in the same doctrine that governs mature infrastructures: segmentation by responsibility across regulated lifecycle flow. Electrical systems separate generation, stabilization, transmission, distribution, and consumption because infrastructure must contain risk and isolate failure. The segmentation is not optional; it is the condition for endurance.

The five-layer Data Grid follows this doctrine:

- Ingestion Consistency establishes source fidelity.
- Engineering Validity enforces structural compatibility.
- Canonical Modeling preserves transmission integrity and optionality.
- Business Component absorbs domain volatility.
- Application Intelligence enables controlled specialization and AI-driven interpretation.

Together they form a regulated flow from reproducible origin to intelligent consumption. The lower three layers constitute the Deterministic Structural Core. Above this core, the Determinism Gradient permits increasing semantic flexibility without compromising structural invariants—mirroring control hierarchies in power systems. The purpose of segmentation is containment. By preventing volatility from flowing downward, the architecture ensures that business change does not rewrite infrastructure and AI experimentation does not destabilize deterministic foundations. Stable infrastructure requires boundary clarity. Boundary clarity requires lifecycle segmentation. The five-layer architecture is therefore not a design preference, but infrastructure doctrine—a principled, lifecycle-spanning partitioning of responsibility that makes robustness, scalability, and AI compatibility structurally possible. Without such segmentation, data systems may function. But they will not endure.

4.2   The Vertical Semantic Elevation View

The horizontal lifecycle architecture governs structural flow. It defines where data enters the infrastructure, how it is stabilized, how it is canonically modeled, and where specialization is permitted. Through lifecycle segmentation, responsibilities are partitioned and volatility is contained. Yet structural layering alone does not fully explain how data matures. It explains movement, but not meaning.

A dataset may pass deterministically through all lifecycle layers and remain technically consumable, while still lacking embedded awareness of its own transformation journey. Records may be cleansed, standardized, modeled, and aggregated without retaining explicit state information about how those transformations occurred. In such systems, lineage must be reconstructed externally. Data quality must be inferred from monitoring dashboards. Governance becomes retrospective rather than intrinsic. The infrastructure functions—but it does not explain itself. This limitation reveals a second architectural requirement. If lifecycle layering governs horizontal movement, semantic elevation governs vertical maturation. Data infrastructure must not only move records across responsibility boundaries; it must progressively encode the meaning accumulated at each stage.

4.2.1   Additive Semantic Accumulation

In communication engineering, a packet ascends the OSI protocol stack while accumulating structured headers. Each protocol layer contributes routing context, sequencing information, integrity verification, and session semantics. The payload itself remains intact, but the packet becomes progressively self-describing. Meaning is layered through encapsulation rather than substitution. Lower-layer information is not destroyed; it is preserved within an expanding semantic envelope. Data infrastructure can adopt the same discipline. As records transition from the Ingestion Consistency Layer to the Engineering Validity Layer, from Canonical Modeling to Business Components, and ultimately to Application Intelligence, they should accumulate structured state markers. These markers may include validation outcomes, transformation identifiers, rule versions, processing timestamps, anomaly flags, semantic readiness classifications, or governance states. These markers are not auxiliary documentation. They are part of the data artifact itself.

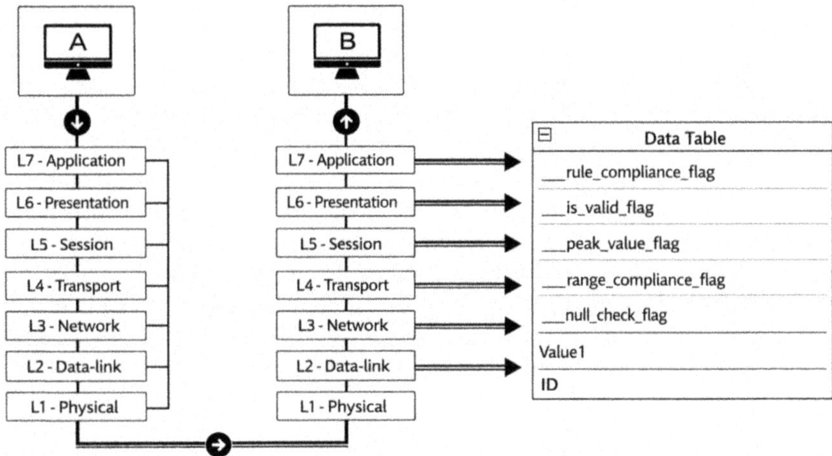

Fig. 4.2 Vertical Semantic Enrichment in Data Infrastructure Inspired by the OSI Model. This diagram highlights how each data lifecycle stage adds structured meaning, similar to how each OSI layer adds protocol headers, preserving context and integrity as data moves upward

Figure 4.2 illustrates this vertical correspondence. On the left, the OSI stack demonstrates progressive protocol encapsulation. On the right, a data table demonstrates additive metadata columns appended as records ascend lifecycle layers. Indicators such as rule compliance flags, validation states, range checks, null verification markers, or transformation identifiers function analogously to protocol headers. They do not overwrite the underlying values. Instead, they form a semantic envelope surrounding them. Each lifecycle stage contributes structured context that remains attached to the record throughout its journey.

4.2.2   From Structural Discipline to Semantic Transparency

The significance of this additive model extends beyond conceptual symmetry. When validation outcomes travel with the data, quality enforcement becomes intrinsic rather than external. When rule identifiers and version numbers are embedded within records, lineage reconstruction becomes native rather than inferential. When semantic readiness states are explicitly encoded, downstream systems—including AI models—can evaluate contextual reliability without consulting detached governance repositories. The record becomes self-describing. Its origin, validation history, and transformation pathway are directly inspectable.

Without progressive semantic encoding, lifecycle architecture remains structurally disciplined but semantically incomplete. Canonical models may preserve relational integrity, yet they do not reveal how individual records achieved their modeled state. Business components may compute domain metrics, but they provide no embedded evidence of the validation journey that preceded them. In such environments, organizations depend on centralized lineage graphs, external reconciliation logs, and documentation artifacts detached from the data itself. These mechanisms are fragile. They require synchronization across systems. They degrade silently when logs are incomplete or when schema evolution disrupts tracking.

Progressive semantic elevation addresses this deficiency by transforming data from passive storage artifacts into carriers of lifecycle intelligence. Each record accumulates a structured state vector reflecting the transformations it has undergone. This state vector is additive, immutable once written, and version-aware. It preserves semantic transparency while maintaining structural determinism. Importantly, this principle does not mandate a specific technology. It mandates a design doctrine: semantic refinement must be additive rather than destructive.

4.2.3   Complementarity with Lifecycle Segmentation

The vertical semantic view complements the horizontal lifecycle architecture. Horizontally, segmentation protects the Deterministic Structural Core from volatility by enforcing responsibility boundaries. Vertically, progressive semantic encoding ensures that abstraction does not erase transparency. Together, these two dimensions produce an infrastructure that is not only layered but intelligible. The system explains its own behavior. It exposes its validation history. It encodes its transformation lineage.

4.2.4   Implications for AI-Augmented Infrastructure

In AI-augmented environments, semantic elevation becomes indispensable. AI systems consume not only values but context. When probabilistic models operate on records stripped of validation state or transformation lineage, uncertainty compounds. Interpretability diminishes. Risk containment weakens. When models operate on semantically enriched records whose lifecycle state is explicitly encoded, interpretability improves and failure boundaries become measurable. Progressive semantic elevation therefore does not merely enhance governance—it enables safe AI integration within deterministic infrastructure constraints. Lifecycle segmentation ensures that data moves safely. Semantic elevation ensures that data remembers how it moved. Only when both dimensions are present does the Data Grid function as true Soft Infrastructure—structurally disciplined, semantically transparent, and prepared for sustained evolution.

4.3 The System Representation and Control View

4.3.1 Infrastructure as a System of Systems

Lifecycle segmentation establishes structural responsibility boundaries. Semantic elevation establishes progressive state encoding. Together, these dimensions ensure that data flows deterministically and that meaning accumulates transparently. Yet neither dimension alone explains how the infrastructure governs and expresses its own operational behavior.

In many modern data environments, transformation logic, orchestration policies, quality thresholds, and governance rules are embedded within procedural code. These behaviors execute, but they are not represented as structured infrastructure state. They are distributed across pipelines, notebooks, scheduler configurations, and runtime scripts. Such systems are operational, but opaque. They can run, yet they cannot be fully inspected, reasoned about, or versioned as coherent infrastructure artifacts. If data is to be treated as infrastructure, this opacity becomes structurally unacceptable. Infrastructure must expose its operational state. It must be governable, auditable, and reproducible. This requirement introduces a third methodological dimension: system representation as data.

Digital systems possess a structural advantage unavailable to physical infrastructure. Their behavior can itself be formalized, stored, and manipulated as structured data. Transformation rules, orchestration intent, freshness constraints, validation policies, and dependency relationships can be expressed declaratively. When such artifacts are structured, version-controlled, and queryable, system behavior transitions from implicit execution to explicit infrastructure state. The paradigm shifts from code-centric execution toward metadata-centric control.

4.3.2 Primary and Secondary Systems

Infrastructure engineering clarifies the necessity of this shift. In electrical grids, the primary system consists of generation facilities, transmission networks, and distribution lines. These components transport energy. Surrounding them are secondary systems—protection relays, monitoring sensors, stabilization controls, and supervisory control networks. Secondary systems do not generate energy; they ensure that the primary system operates safely and predictably.

Data infrastructure follows analogous logic. Structured data tables form the primary system—they transport and persist enterprise information. Quality enforcement, governance frameworks, orchestration engines, lineage capture systems, observability pipelines, and access controls form the secondary system. They do not produce data; they regulate and protect its flow.

When secondary behaviors are implemented solely as procedural code, they remain external to the infrastructure state. Governance depends on implementation discipline rather than enforceable structure. Orchestration logic entangles with transformation code. Auditing requires log reconstruction rather than state inspection. By representing secondary system behavior as structured data, infrastructure control becomes part of the infrastructure fabric. Configuration tables encode transformation intent. Rule registries define validation policies. Dependency graphs become materialized data artifacts. Execution states are captured as structured telemetry. The infrastructure becomes introspectable.

The result is a Data Infrastructure System of Systems (SoS):

- The Primary System: structured data assets (tables, canonical models).
- The Secondary System: governance, validation, orchestration, telemetry, and control logic—represented as structured metadata.
- The Control Fabric: declarative reconciliation mechanisms aligning intent and execution.

The infrastructure no longer merely processes data. It represents, governs, and reasons about itself.

4.3.3   From Execution to Declarative Control

Representing behavior as structured data fundamentally alters the execution model. In code-centric environments, operational behavior is embedded in imperative programs. Understanding system state requires reading scripts and reconstructing implicit logic. Control is distributed across runtime artifacts. In a metadata-centric model, the desired infrastructure state is declared explicitly. Execution engines reconcile observed runtime conditions against declared configuration state. Execution becomes deterministic state reconciliation rather than procedural invocation. This control fabric consists of four conceptual strata:

- Intent Declaration: Transformation specifications, validation policies, freshness rules, and dependency structures are encoded as structured metadata.
- Divergence Evaluation: Declared intent is continuously compared against observed system state.
- Reconciliation Execution: Standardized execution mechanisms resolve divergence and restore alignment.
- Telemetry Recording: Execution outcomes are captured as structured metadata, forming persistent operational memory.

The upper portion in Fig. 4.3 depicts the legacy paradigm: orchestration triggers embedded code; logic is opaque; outputs emerge from execution chains whose internal state must be inferred. The lower portion depicts the metadata-driven paradigm: intent is declared in structured configuration artifacts; orchestration topology is formalized; runtime state is recorded; telemetry forms persistent memory. "What to do," "how to do," and "what happened" become explicit infrastructure state

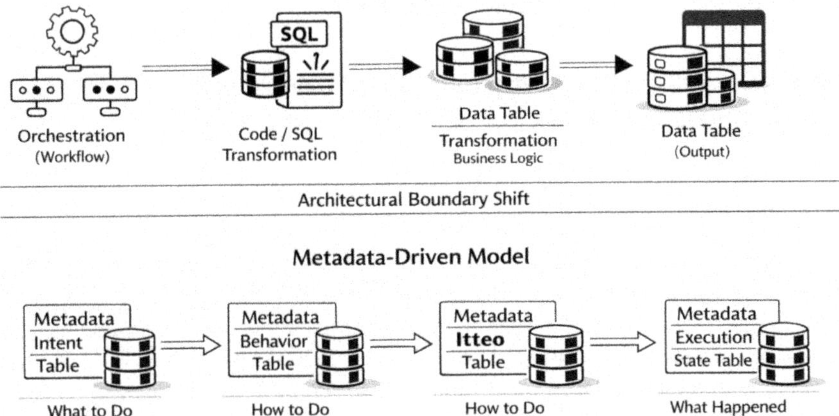

Fig. 4.3 From code-embedded execution to metadata-driven declarative control in infrastructure operations

rather than implicit script behavior. This shift is structural. Control logic converges with data assets into a unified representational substrate.

4.3.4   Infrastructure Self-Representation and Digital Twin

When transformation intent, orchestration topology, governance policy, lineage relationships, and execution telemetry are all represented as structured data, infrastructure achieves recursive self-representation. The platform no longer merely manages data. The platform becomes data.

Topology, dependency graphs, rule versions, and execution histories become explicit, queryable infrastructure states. The system can reason about its own configuration and operational condition. This constitutes the foundation for a Digital Twin of the Data Infrastructure. In this model, infrastructure is not merely monitored externally; it is internally representable. The distinction between managed assets and managing systems collapses into a unified metadata fabric. Only under such conditions can deterministic governance and analyzable evolution become structurally guaranteed.

4.4   The AI Boundary and Control View

4.4.1   *Deterministic Infrastructure and Controlled Augmentation*

Lifecycle segmentation protects structural boundaries. Semantic elevation preserves transparency. System representation formalizes governable execution. These three dimensions collectively establish deterministic infrastructure foundations. The final question is how AI integrates within this structure. AI systems are probabilistic inference engines. Infrastructure systems are deterministic control environments. The issue is not whether AI should participate, but where its boundary lies. When system behavior is structured, additive, and version-controlled, AI can operate safely within declared control interfaces. AI may assist in anomaly detection, optimization recommendations, transformation suggestions, and adaptive scheduling. However, execution authority remains bound to a versioned, structured infrastructure state. AI functions as a constrained co-processor, not a structural authority. Control engineering principles guide this boundary:

- Execution intent must remain declarative and versioned.
- AI outputs must be testable before reconciliation.
- Divergence detection must remain deterministic.
- Rollback must be structurally possible.
- Observability must be preserved independently of AI inference.

When AI is allowed to modify structural layers—particularly within the Deterministic Structural Core—uncertainty propagates uncontrollably. Probabilistic inference must not overwrite deterministic origin, structural validation, or canonical transmission layers. Instead, AI operates above protected structural cores, within bounded adaptation domains. The Determinism Gradient applies here as well:

- Strong determinism at infrastructure foundation.
- Controlled flexibility at semantic layers.
- Probabilistic experimentation at application boundaries.

This boundary ensures that AI enhances infrastructure without destabilizing it.

4.4.2   *Infrastructure Determinism and Evolution*

When operational behavior is representable as structured data, change becomes analyzable rather than disruptive. Governance becomes enforceable rather than advisory. Infrastructure evolves through configuration state transitions rather than uncontrolled code modification. This leads to a general infrastructure principle:

- Within control and observability domains, operational behavior must be representable as structured data.
- Systems built on this foundation are not toolchains; they are infrastructure systems. They are self-describing, deterministically governable, and capable of controlled adaptation.

Only under such structural conditions can data infrastructure function as resilient Soft Infrastructure for the AI-native industrial era. Without explicit system representation and explicit AI boundaries, digital systems may operate. But they will not remain governable.

4.5 Further Reading

To extend the System of Systems and AI Boundary perspectives developed in this chapter—particularly the transition from code-centric execution to metadata-centric control, the formalization of infrastructure as structured state, recursive self-representation through digital twins, and the establishment of deterministic control boundaries for AI augmentation—the following academic resources provide complementary theoretical grounding and engineering patterns. These works focus on declarative infrastructure control, system-of-systems thinking, digital twin formalization, layered architecture rigor, and safe integration of intelligent automation.

- Bass, L., Clements, P., & Kazman, R. (2021). Software Architecture in Practice (4th ed.). Addison-Wesley.

  - Annotation: This foundational text articulates architectural tactics for modifiability, observability, and layered system design. It emphasizes separation of concerns, explicit architectural representation, and traceable quality attributes. The discussion of architectural views and runtime state models aligns directly with the metadata-centric control paradigm and the formalization of infrastructure behavior as analyzable state rather than embedded code.

- Garlan, D., & Shaw, M. (1994). "An Introduction to Software Architecture." Advances in Software Engineering and Knowledge Engineering.

  - Annotation: A seminal work introducing architectural styles and formal system composition. It provides theoretical foundations for understanding systems as structured compositions of interacting components—a precursor to modern system-of-systems engineering. Its emphasis on explicit architectural constraints supports the chapter's doctrine of enforceable lifecycle and control boundaries.

- Jamshidi, M. (2009). System of Systems Engineering: Innovations for the 21st Century. Wiley.

  – Annotation: A comprehensive treatment of System of Systems (SoS) theory, including hierarchical control, interoperability constraints, and emergent behavior containment. This work underpins the conceptual framing of data infrastructure as a governed SoS composed of primary data assets and secondary stabilizing subsystems.

- Lee, J., Bagheri, B., & Kao, H. (2015). "A Cyber-Physical Systems Architecture for Industry 4.0-Based Manufacturing Systems." Manufacturing Letters.

  – Annotation: Introduces layered cyber-physical system architectures integrating sensing, modeling, control, and analytics. The paper's structured separation between physical assets and supervisory intelligence mirrors the separation between deterministic structural cores and higher-level adaptive AI layers in data infrastructure.

- Kreutz, D., Ramos, F., Verissimo, P., et al. (2015). "Software-Defined Networking: A Comprehensive Survey." Proceedings of the IEEE.

  – Annotation: Explores the architectural decoupling of control planes from data planes in network systems. The separation between declarative control logic and packet forwarding parallels the metadata-driven control fabric described in this chapter, where infrastructure behavior is declared and reconciled rather than embedded in execution paths.

- Cloutier, R., Verma, D., Nilchiani, R., et al. (2015). "The Concept of Reference Architectures." Systems Engineering.

  – Annotation: Discusses reference architectures as formalized structural blueprints for complex systems. The paper emphasizes boundary clarity, responsibility partitioning, and architectural invariants—core principles underlying lifecycle segmentation and deterministic infrastructure doctrine.

- Batty, M. (2018). "Digital Twins." Environment and Planning B: Urban Analytics and City Science.

  – Annotation: Examines digital twins as dynamic, data-driven representations capable of simulation and real-time synchronization. While focused on urban systems, the conceptual treatment of recursive representation supports the extension of digital twin theory to data infrastructure itself.

- Fuller, A., Fan, Z., Day, C., & Barlow, C. (2020). "Digital Twin: Enabling Technologies, Challenges and Open Research." IEEE Access.

  – Annotation: Reviews enabling technologies for digital twins, emphasizing synchronization, bidirectional feedback, and lifecycle monitoring. The paper's articulation of twin-state alignment resonates with the metadata-centric reconciliation model and infrastructure self-representation described in this chapter.

- Rahman, M., & Kayes, A. (2022). "Explainable Artificial Intelligence for Cyber-Physical Systems." ACM Computing Surveys.

- – Annotation: Surveys XAI methods within controlled system environments, stressing interpretability, bounded autonomy, and auditability. The discussion reinforces the necessity of deterministic control interfaces and explicit AI boundaries when integrating probabilistic systems into infrastructure contexts.

- NIST (2023). AI Risk Management Framework (AI RMF 1.0). National Institute of Standards and Technology.

  - – Annotation: Establishes governance principles for trustworthy AI, including traceability, accountability, and risk containment. The framework aligns with the chapter's argument that AI must operate within deterministic infrastructure constraints rather than redefine structural layers.

Collectively, these works reinforce the chapter's central thesis: infrastructure maturity requires explicit representation of operational behavior, disciplined separation between primary and secondary systems, and enforceable control boundaries for intelligent augmentation. By synthesizing system-of-systems theory, software architecture formalism, digital twin modeling, and AI governance research, the Data Grid emerges not as a tooling pattern but as an infrastructure doctrine—one in which structure, state, and control converge into a unified, metadata-driven foundation capable of deterministic execution and safe evolution in AI-native environments.

Chapter 5
Data Modeling

Abstract This chapter redefines data modeling as an infrastructure discipline grounded in lifecycle responsibility rather than reporting convenience. It proposes a layered modeling framework in which foundational layers maintain structural consistency and semantic integrity, while upper layers accommodate business variability under controlled boundaries. The chapter outlines architectural mandates for immutability, canonical representation, normalization, and volatility isolation. Through case studies involving metadata-based transformation representation and graph-driven entity resolution, it demonstrates how disciplined modeling supports reliability, governance, and controlled AI integration. The chapter positions modeling as the semantic backbone of the infrastructure.

Keyword Infrastructure-grade data modeling · Deterministic structural core · Semantic contract enforcement · Transformation-as-Data · AI boundary engineering · Graphtheoretic identity resolution

Having established the cross-disciplinary blueprint of the Data Grid in Chapter 4, we now transition from structural doctrine to semantic implementation. If Chap. 4 defined how infrastructure must be segmented—how data flows across lifecycle responsibilities, how semantics accumulate additively, and how system behavior becomes representable—then Chap. 5 formalizes how enterprise data should be modeled inside those boundaries.

Data modeling is not treated here as a downstream analytic task. It is an infrastructure discipline. Within the Data Grid paradigm, modeling decisions are not merely choices of schema style or reporting convenience; they directly determine system stability, evolvability, semantic interoperability, auditability, and AI compatibility. Historically, many enterprise data systems evolved around application-driven demands. Pipelines were optimized for immediate reporting needs; business logic was injected close to ingestion; and metrics were defined independently across teams and domains. While such approaches can create short-term agility, they produce long-term structural fragility: duplicated semantic contracts, tightly coupled pipelines,

Z. T. Lee, *The Data Grid*, SpringerBriefs in Computer Science,
https://doi.org/10.1007/978-3-032-25004-9_5

ambiguous grains, and inconsistent interpretation surfaces. In AI-integrated environments, these weaknesses are amplified. Modern AI systems are probabilistic by nature: they can accelerate transformation authoring and analytical exploration, but they do not inherently guarantee structural correctness, traceability, or reproducibility. For this reason, modeling must establish deterministic boundaries. The structural core of enterprise data must remain governed, versioned, and auditable. AI may assist within constrained domains, but it cannot replace architectural discipline. Data modeling therefore serves two simultaneous objectives:

- Formalize semantic contracts across lifecycle layers (grain, identity, versioning, dependency structure, lineage).
- Define deterministic control surfaces for safe AI augmentation (explicit boundaries, testability, rollback, and invariant protection).

To remain consistent with Chap. 4, we express modeling responsibilities through the same five-layer lifecycle segmentation. The first three layers constitute the Deterministic Structural Core (DSC); the upper two layers absorb volatility and enable specialization under the Determinism Gradient.

5.1 Ingestion Consistency Layer—Source-Faithful Truth

The Ingestion Consistency Layer (or Bronze layer in medallion structure) is the immutable historical archive of the Data Grid. Its purpose is preservation, not interpretation. At this boundary, the infrastructure acts as a faithful recorder of upstream system behavior, ensuring that the enterprise maintains a reproducible origin state for replay, forensic reconstruction, and time-consistent traceability. This layer corresponds directly to the DSC's first segment: deterministic origin. To satisfy its mandate, Bronze modeling follows five infrastructure requirements:

- Mandate 1—Absolute Immutability (Append-Only History). Data must be stored as received using append-focused persistence that preserves the full change history. Without immutability, the grid loses its forensic record and can no longer replay transformations when downstream modeling errors are discovered.
- Mandate 2—Preservation of Technical Provenance ("Protocol Headers"). Every record must carry durable ingestion metadata: source identifiers, ingestion timestamps, sequence/version markers, and other technical lineage anchors. If these headers are missing, lineage collapses into inference, and auditing—including auditing AI-assisted decisions—becomes structurally unreliable.
- Mandate 3—Zero Business Logic Injection. No KPI logic, domain deduplication rules, early enrichment, or application-driven reshaping is permitted. At most, transformations should be limited to technical necessities that preserve fidelity (e.g., file format optimization, schema capture without semantic reinterpretation).

- Mandate 4—Resilience to Malformed and Inconsistent Inputs. The ingestion boundary must capture upstream exhaust even when it is malformed, duplicated, or inconsistent with the current schema. Rejecting such records causes irreversible "signal dropout," preventing future diagnosis of upstream system behavior.
- Mandate 5—High-Fidelity Granularity. The captured grain must match the source grain; no pre-aggregation or summarization is allowed. If granularity is lost here, the system irreversibly destroys fine-grained truth, forcing downstream analytics and AI to operate on "blurred" signals.

In short, Bronze is not "raw tables" as a convenience layer. It is the enterprise's provable origin state. If Bronze is not strictly source-faithful, the remainder of the grid may operate—but it cannot be defended as infrastructure.

5.2 Engineering Validity Layer—Technical Trust and Interoperability

If Bronze establishes deterministic origin, the Engineering Validity Layer (or Silver layer in medallion structure) establishes deterministic interoperability. In the infrastructure analogy, Silver functions as the substation: it stabilizes raw signals into an enterprise-compatible technical standard without injecting domain interpretation. It corresponds to the DSC's second segment: deterministic compatibility. The governing principle of Silver modeling is deterministic transformation. Every operation must be reproducible and independent of business semantics. Silver is not the layer of "opinions." It is where technical trust is engineered. Silver modeling adheres to five mandates:

- Mandate 1—Canonical Schema Enforcement and Type Normalization. All incoming data must be cast into standardized enterprise technical formats (e.g., ISO time standards, consistent null handling, unified numeric/boolean encoding). Failure to normalize creates persistent impedance for downstream composition, automation, and AI reasoning.
- Mandate 2—Deterministic Deduplication and Technical Reconciliation. Duplicates, late-arriving corrections, and ordering anomalies must be resolved using fixed technical rules grounded in version markers, technical timestamps, or deterministic precedence. Without this reconciliation, downstream metrics and features become poisoned by "signal echoes."
- Mandate 3—Exclusion of Business Semantics and KPIs. Silver must remain insulated from business-definition logic. When KPI logic enters Silver, foundational stability collapses into specialization, forcing costly reprocessing when definitions evolve.
- Mandate 4—Multi-Source Alignment and Identity Harmonization. Records from disparate systems must be aligned into a common structural framework so that the same real-world entity is technically representable across sources.

Without alignment, the enterprise grid becomes semantically blind to cross-system journeys.

- Mandate 5—Freshness Semantics and Temporal Consistency Signals. Each dataset must expose clear freshness and latency metadata so consumers and automated agents can reason about timeliness deterministically. Without this, the system enters temporal blindness, enabling decisions (human or AI) on stale data under false assumptions.

Silver, therefore, is the engineering layer that makes data technically stable and joinable at enterprise scale—without deciding what the business "means."

5.3 Canonical Modeling Layer—Enterprise Semantic Backbone

If Silver stabilizes technical trust, the Canonical Modeling Layer (or Gold layer in medallion structure) establishes semantic trust: the enterprise's reusable representation of business truth. In the infrastructure analogy, Gold acts as the high-voltage transmission backbone—optimized for reuse and composability rather than local consumption convenience. This corresponds to the DSC's third segment: deterministic semantic primitives. Gold models are expressed as stable business entities (Dimensions) and atomic business events (Facts). The design philosophy is universal composability: downstream systems—dashboards, operational services, external interfaces, and AI agents—should be able to integrate with canonical structures and obtain consistent, high-fidelity semantics.

5.3.1 Normalization as Infrastructure Doctrine

Gold is aligned with classical normalization (1NF/2NF/3NF), but not as a database-theory exercise. Here, normalization functions as an infrastructure discipline: it creates the smallest stable semantic building blocks, minimizing future rework and maximizing recombination under evolving requirements. Premature denormalization at Gold embeds application assumptions into the backbone and turns infrastructure into product.

5.3.2 Architectural Mandates for Canonical Modeling

To function as the authoritative semantic backbone, Gold modeling follows five mandates:

- Mandate 1—Explicit Grain Definition (1NF as Semantic Atomicity). Every table must have a strictly defined grain: what a row represents, at what level of observation. Without explicit grain, aggregation becomes non-deterministic, causing inconsistency across metrics and AI features.
- Mandate 2—Stable Identity Anchors and Key Separation (2NF as Dependency Integrity). Surrogate keys anchor identity independent of volatile operational identifiers. Business identifiers may change; structural joins must not depend on them.
- Mandate 3—Explicit Historical Versioning (Temporal Truth as First-Class). Gold must distinguish historical truth from current-state representations. Overwrites destroy back-testing, longitudinal analysis, and causal inference—especially damaging for AI training and evaluation.
- Mandate 4—Strict Fact–Dimension Separation (3NF as Dependency Isolation). Facts contain measures aligned to declared grain; descriptive attributes belong in dimensions. Mixing attributes with measures creates hidden transitive dependencies and collapses composability.
- Mandate 5—Domain-Agnostic Genericity (Universal Reusability). Gold must model stable enterprise entities—not application schemas. Application-driven schemas introduce semantic coupling and reduce the ability to reuse intelligence across domains.

Gold is not designed to answer today's dashboard fastest. Gold is designed to remain valid when the dashboards, KPIs, and AI use cases change.

5.4 Business Component Layer—Volatility Absorption and Decision Semantics

Above the DSC lies the Business Component Layer: the volatility buffer where domain composition, KPI semantics, reusable business views, and controlled denormalization are permitted. This layer exists because business meaning evolves. Embedding volatile semantics into canonical models contaminates the backbone and forces systemic rebuilds. In practice, this layer often materializes what can be described as semantic delivery products: curated metric libraries, composite domain views, and decision-aligned aggregations derived primarily from Gold.

- Principle 1—Dependency on the Gold Backbone. Platinum should be derived primarily from Gold (and only exceptionally from lower layers under explicit governance). This preserves semantic coherence and prevents parallel definitions.
- Principle 2—Controlled Denormalization and Business-Aligned Grain. Platinum may intentionally compose across grains and denormalize for usability and performance, but such deviation must remain traceable and bounded.

- Principle 3—Functional Dependency as a Practical Integrity Boundary. Even when 1NF/3NF constraints are relaxed for delivery efficiency, preserving functional dependency discipline (often approximated as a 2NF-like baseline) helps prevent semantic drift and hidden coupling.
- Principle 4—Product-Like Evolution. Delivery models are expected to evolve iteratively with business questions. Their lifecycle should be managed as products—versioned, documented, and replaceable—without destabilizing the canonical backbone.

This layer is where the enterprise converts canonical truth into decision-ready interpretations—without rewriting infrastructure.

5.5 Application Intelligence Layer—Interfaces for Analytics and AI Consumption

The Application Intelligence Layer includes dashboards, feature tables, ML training datasets, decision interfaces, and workflow-specific data products. This is the most specialized and volatile layer. Variability is not a flaw here—it is the point. However, variability must not flow downward. This layer operationalizes the Determinism Gradient defined in Chap. 4:

- Strong determinism in Bronze/Silver/Gold (DSC)
- Controlled flexibility in Platinum (business volatility buffer)
- Probabilistic experimentation and specialization at the application boundary

In AI-driven settings, this boundary is non-negotiable. AI systems may generate features, propose transformations, and optimize schedules, but they must not overwrite deterministic foundations. Application-layer models can move fast, fail safely, and iterate—because rollback and lineage remain anchored to the deterministic core.

Across these five layers, data modeling becomes the mechanism by which the Data Grid enforces semantic contracts, controls volatility propagation, and exposes deterministic boundaries for safe AI augmentation. The lower three layers establish a provable semantic backbone; the upper two layers deliver decision usability and AI-ready specialization without contaminating infrastructure invariants. If Chap. 4 presented the blueprint of soft infrastructure, Chap. 5 operationalizes its semantic discipline: truth is preserved, compatibility is engineered, canon is stabilized, business meaning is composed safely, and intelligent applications are enabled without collapsing determinism.

5.6 Case Study

The preceding sections of this chapter established the structural doctrine of data modeling within the Data Grid: deterministic origin preservation, engineering validity enforcement, canonical semantic backbone construction, volatility isolation, and controlled application specialization. Those principles define where modeling responsibilities reside and why boundaries must be maintained. However, infrastructure doctrine alone does not resolve the practical engineering challenges that arise within and across these layers.

This section introduces three focused case studies designed to operationalize key cross-disciplinary principles discussed in Chaps. 3 and 4. Rather than demonstrating how to construct layered tables—an activity that follows directly from adherence to the defined modeling mandates—these cases address tactical modeling challenges that emerge within the lifecycle architecture. They illustrate how theoretical constructs such as system-of-systems thinking, metadata-driven representation, AI boundary control, and graph-theoretic reasoning translate into concrete engineering practice. Each case intentionally targets problems that may occur in different lifecycle domains. Some are situated within the Engineering Validity Layer (Silver), others within the Canonical Modeling Layer (Gold), and still others at the interface between the Business Component and Application Intelligence layers. Their purpose is not to redefine the layered structure, but to demonstrate how disciplined infrastructure principles guide implementation decisions inside it.

The three case studies are as follows: Case Study 1—Data Logic as Data: Building the Digital Twin of Data Transformations. This example demonstrates how data processing logic can be transformed from procedural code into structured metadata representations. By encoding transformation rules, validation policies, and orchestration intent as relational artifacts, we construct a digital twin of the data logic itself. This operationalizes the System Representation methodology introduced in Chap. 4 and establishes a deterministic control surface for infrastructure behavior. Case Study 2—Defining and Enforcing AI Boundaries in Data Modeling. Building upon the first case, this example illustrates how AI can safely assist in generating or refining transformation logic without violating deterministic infrastructure constraints. It shows how versioned metadata, validation gates, and reconciliation mechanisms define explicit boundaries between probabilistic assistance and authoritative execution. The focus is not on AI capability, but on boundary governance. Case Study 3— Graph-Theoretic Identity Resolution for Sparse and Heterogeneous Data. The final case applies graph theory to address entity deduplication and identification across sparse, multi-source datasets. Rather than relying solely on rule-based matching or simplistic key alignment, graph connectivity analysis enables robust resolution of loosely connected or partially overlapping identities. This example demonstrates how cross-disciplinary reasoning—specifically system-of-systems modeling and network theory—can be applied tactically within data modeling challenges at the Silver and Gold layers.

Together, these case studies illustrate that data modeling in the Data Grid extends beyond schema design. It encompasses the representation of system behavior, the governance of AI augmentation, and the resolution of complex structural ambiguities through formal methods. By grounding abstract principles in executable examples and code artifacts, we demonstrate how infrastructure doctrine translates into operational engineering practice—without compromising lifecycle segmentation or deterministic foundations.

5.6.1 Transformation-As-Data: The Logical Digital Twin of the Data Grid

Figure 5.1 presents the schema of the transformation_rules_configuration table. At first glance, it appears to be a straightforward configuration structure: it defines source tables, target tables, join predicates, transformation logic, and filtering clauses. Yet structurally, it represents a far more significant shift. It operationalizes the third methodological dimension introduced in Chapter 4—System Representation as Data—and concretizes the system-of-systems doctrine at the core of this book.

The problem addressed here is architectural rather than technical. In conventional data environments, transformation logic exists as procedural code: SQL scripts, orchestration DAGs, or embedded notebook logic. Even in so-called configuration-driven systems, YAML or JSON files remain external artifacts interpreted by runtime engines. The system can query the data it produces, but it cannot query—within the same deterministic substrate—the logic that produced it. Lineage must be reconstructed, governance must be inferred, and execution intent remains opaque. The infrastructure operates, yet it does not represent itself.

From the system-of-systems perspective articulated in Chap. 4, this separation is structurally unstable. Mature infrastructures integrate their supervisory systems with their primary transmission systems. Electrical grids embed control and monitoring layers within the same architectural fabric that transports energy. The primary system moves resources; the secondary system governs and stabilizes that movement. They are distinct in responsibility, but unified in representation.

The configuration table shown in Fig. 5.1 collapses this gap. Each row encodes a unit of transformation intent: the source lineage anchor, the declarative join semantics, the column-level transformation expression, the target projection, and optional filtering constraints. These are not parsed scripts; they are relational declarations. The manufacturing logic of the Data Grid is stored as structured data inside the grid itself.

This structural move transforms transformation logic into a Logical Digital Twin of the data manufacturing process. The twin does not simulate business behavior; it

```sql
%sql
CREATE TABLE transformation_rules_configuration (
  target_table STRING
    COMMENT 'Fully qualified target table name.
    The executor will build and write ONE output table per distinct target_table value',
  source_table STRING
    COMMENT 'Source table providing data for transformation.
    Rows with empty join_columns indicate the base (driving) table.
    Other rows represent lookup or reference tables to be joined.',
  join_columns STRING
    COMMENT 'Full SQL join predicate between base table and source_table.
    This field is treated as a declarative SQL expression, not parsed or decomposed.
    Supports nested struct paths (a.b), multiple conditions, and AND logic.
    The executor only rewrites table prefixes to internal aliases.',
  source_column STRING
    COMMENT 'Source column or nested struct path read AS-IS from source_table.
    No inference or column-name rewriting is performed by the executor.',
  transform_logic STRING
    COMMENT 'Optional transformation applied to source_column.
    Typically a SQL UDF with no arguments, such as unix_ms_to_date().
    Leave NULL or empty for direct projection of the source value.',
  target_column STRING
    COMMENT 'Final output column name in the target table schema.
    This value is explicitly defined by the configuration author.
    Must be unique (case-insensitive) within each target_table.',
  filter_where_caluse STRING
    COMMENT 'Optional WHERE clause applied after all joins and before final projection.
    This field is treated as raw SQL.
    Leave NULL if no row-level filtering is required.'
) USING DELTA
COMMENT 'Config-driven transformation rules.
  This table declaratively defines source lineage, join semantics,
  column-level transformations, and target schemas for self-service execution.';
```

Fig. 5.1 Transformation logic configuration data table—physical schema of the transformation logic configuration data table, illustrating how data manufacturing rules are stored as queryable, structured metadata

mirrors the structural mechanics of how data flows from source to target across life-cycle layers. Because the logic is stored relationally, it becomes queryable, versionable, and auditable using the same deterministic infrastructure that governs enterprise data. The system can now ask—in SQL—not only "what data exists," but "how is this data produced," "which upstream elements feed this metric," or "what transformations define this column."

In terms of Chap. 4's framework, this design formally integrates the Secondary System—governance, transformation rules, dependency structure—into the same representational domain as the Primary System of data assets. The control fabric becomes declarative. Execution is no longer the invocation of opaque scripts but the reconciliation of the declared transformation state with observed runtime state. Infrastructure behavior transitions from implicit procedure to explicit configuration state.

The importance of this case study is not that it replaces code with tables. Its significance lies in restoring infrastructural symmetry. When transformation logic is representable as data, lineage becomes declarative rather than inferred. Governance becomes enforceable rather than advisory. Change becomes a controlled state transition rather than an uncontrolled code modification. The Data Grid acquires memory of how data is manufactured, not merely the results of that manufacturing.

This is the practical realization of the system-of-systems doctrine. The grid no longer merely processes data; it represents and governs its own behavior. In doing so, it establishes the deterministic substrate required for observability, automation, and—as the next case will demonstrate—bounded AI augmentation.

5.6.2 AI Boundary Engineering: Black-Box Assistance Under White-Box Control

This section approaches data system construction from a complementary methodological perspective: integrating artificial intelligence while explicitly defining its operational boundaries within data infrastructure. As AI-assisted development tools become increasingly capable, a growing share of engineering tasks—especially those involving descriptive specifications or pattern-to-code translation—can be partially automated. The architectural question is therefore no longer whether AI is useful, but how it should be placed within an infrastructure system whose primary obligation is determinism, reliability, and governance.

A foundational property of AI systems is that their outputs are probabilistic. Even when empirical accuracy is high, correctness cannot be guaranteed in all cases. From an engineering perspective, this introduces uncertainty that must be explicitly bound and actively managed. Infrastructure systems cannot rely on unbounded probabilistic behavior as a primary control mechanism. Instead, uncertainty must be made observable, testable, and containable by design. The boundary question can be stated directly:

- Where can AI operate safely under explicit verification?
- Where must deterministic, human-controlled logic remain the source of truth?

To answer this question, we distinguish between white-box required domains and black-box acceptable domains within the Data Grid. This distinction is not philosophical. It follows directly from systems engineering and control theory: components are governed differently depending on controllability, testability, and failure tolerance.

Figure 5.2 illustrates a conventional, code-centric implementation of transformation logic. The logic exists as procedural SQL, tightly coupled to a specific implementation artifact. While readable to engineers, it remains operationally opaque at infrastructure scale: lineage is not native, governance is external, and the transformation definition is not structurally integrated into the grid. Building on the Transformation-as-Data paradigm established in the previous case study, Fig. 5.2

```sql
SELECT
  sha2(CAST(id AS STRING), 256) AS unique_id,
  upper(name) AS standardized_name,
  CASE
    WHEN phone IS NULL THEN NULL
    ELSE
      CASE
        WHEN
          length(regexp_replace(phone, '[^0-9]', '')) = 10
        THEN
          concat(
            '+1 ',
            substr(regexp_replace(phone, '[^0-9]', ''), 1, 3),
            ' ',
            substr(regexp_replace(phone, '[^0-9]', ''), 4, 3),
            ' ',
            substr(regexp_replace(phone, '[^0-9]', ''), 7, 4)
          )
        ELSE NULL
      END
  END AS standardized_phone,
  CASE
    WHEN
      regexp_like(lower(trim(email)), '^[A-Za-z0-9._%+-]+@[A-Za-z0-9.-]+\.[A-Za-z]{2,}$')
    THEN
      lower(trim(email))
    ELSE NULL
  END AS standardized_email
FROM
  entity;
```

Fig. 5.2 The code based logic

shows the structural inversion: the transformation logic is represented as data rather than code. Each row captures the target table, the source lineage anchor, and the transformation instruction. Notably, the transformation logic itself can be represented as either executable expressions or controlled natural-language specifications that remain inside the metadata fabric. This shift is essential for AI integration because it converts an otherwise opaque engineering activity into a controlled, versioned interface. Once transformation intent is represented through structured metadata, the infrastructure can separate responsibilities according to what must remain deterministic and what can tolerate bounded uncertainty. The result is a control methodology grounded in the third and fourth dimensions of Chapter 4: system representation and controlled AI augmentation.

White-Box Domain—Deterministic Infrastructure Control

Certain components must remain explicitly human-controlled and fully observable. These components form the macro-structural skeleton of the Data Grid. They include end-to-end lineage, source-to-target relationships, column-level mapping, transformation topology, and data contract enforcement. In Chapter 4 terms, these elements belong to the deterministic control surface of the grid. They are difficult to validate exhaustively because their correctness is global rather than local: errors propagate across domains, validation cost is high, and many choices become one-time architectural commitments. If AI were allowed to generate or modify these structures autonomously, end-to-end validation would become prohibitively expensive, and governance would become fragile. For this reason, these elements must remain white-box: represented as structured configuration data, versioned, reviewable, and queryable by design. The system must always be able to explain itself at the structural level, independent of any AI component.

Black-Box Domain—Testable, Function-Bounded Transformation Logic

In contrast, many transformation operations can be treated as bounded engineering functions. They typically have clear input/output boundaries, deterministic expectations, and localized failure impact. These properties make them suitable for verification through unit tests, schema constraints, and deterministic data validation rules. Under these conditions, AI can be safely used as an implementation accelerator: the internal generation process may remain black-box, but correctness is enforced through white-box verification. This is the critical inversion. AI does not become the source of truth. It becomes a bounded generator whose outputs must pass deterministic acceptance criteria before being activated.

AI as a Bounded Co-Processor in the Metadata Twin

Figure 5.3 demonstrates how this boundary is operationalized. The Databricks ai_ query() function is used to translate a natural-language instruction into an executable SQL expression. The prompt is intentionally constrained: it requires the model to return only a SQL snippet and to output a deterministic fallback value if the instruction cannot be translated. In this example, the instruction—"Format the phone number in E.164 style (e.g., + 1 123 456 7890)"—is converted into a concrete SQL expression that can be inserted into the transformation rule shown in Fig. 5.4.

The important point is where this AI-generated logic resides and how it is activated. It is not injected directly into an opaque pipeline. Instead, it becomes a candidate transformation specification inside the structured metadata fabric. At that point, the deterministic infrastructure retains control. The system can validate the generated expression against test cases, sample datasets, schema constraints, and downstream compatibility requirements. If validation fails, the change is rejected or revised and re-tested. The failure is locally contained and reversible.

This is precisely the distinction between black-box acceptable and white-box required domains. Black-box generation is acceptable where failures are detectable, reversible, and locally contained. White-box control is required where failures are

target_table	source_table	source_column_name	AI_transform_logic	target_column_name
processed_entity	entity	id	Generate a stable key by hashing the id.	unique_id
processed_entity	entity	name	Convert the value to uppercase.	standardized_name
processed_entity	entity	phone	Format the phone number in E.164 style (e.g., +1 123 456 7890).	standardized_phone
processed_entity	entity	email	Normalize the email address (trim and lowercase) and validate its format.	standardized_email

Fig. 5.3 The structured data based logic

```
SELECT
  ai_query(
    'databricks-gpt-5-mini',
    'Task: Convert the following natural language instruction into a Databricks SQL expression fragment.
    Context Column: 1 123 456 7890
    Instruction: Format the phone number in E.164 style (e.g., +1 123 456 7890)
    Requirements:
    1. Return ONLY the SQL code snippet.
    2. If the instruction is non-sense or cannot be translated, return ''UNRECOGNIZED''.
    3. No explanations, no markdown, no preamble.'
  ) as result
```

See performance (1)

Table ˅   +

result

CONCAT('+', regexp_extract(context_column, '^([0-9]{1})'), ' ', regexp_replace(regexp_extract(context_column, '^[0-9]+\\s+([0-9]{3})\\s+([0-9]{3})\\s+([0-9]{4})$'), '\\s+', ' '))

Fig. 5.4 Translate natural language to executable sql statement (using databricks ai_query)

systemic, expensive to validate, and difficult to unwind. Seen through the lens of control theory, the boundary is governed by two variables: degree of controllability and tolerance for failure. AI should be applied where behavior can be bounded through deterministic verification and rollback. It must be restricted where correctness depends on global architectural commitments and where error propagation would compromise the structural integrity of the grid.

This framework provides a practical methodology for designing AI-era data infrastructure with explicit trust boundaries. The next case study reinforces the same philosophy from a different cross-disciplinary angle. In entity deduplication, one can either rely on probabilistic fuzzy matching or adopt deterministic graph-based identity resolution. In high-stakes environments where fuzzy outcomes are unacceptable, graph connectivity provides the stronger infrastructure-grade solution.

5.6.3   Graph-Based Entity Unification in Sparse Industrial Data

Modern industrial data systems repeatedly encounter an identity problem that traditional relational modeling assumes away. Classical warehouse design relies on stable global identifiers—primary keys that persist across systems and foreign keys that reliably join records into coherent entities. In practice, those "hard links" are frequently unavailable. Privacy constraints remove or mask identifiers, legacy systems encode identity inconsistently, and many operational datasets contain only partial or low-frequency attributes. The result is an infrastructure-level identity crisis: the semantic backbone may be well designed, yet entity continuity cannot be maintained because records cannot be confidently joined.

Figure 5.5 frames this contrast. On the left, traditional approaches depend on identifier-based joins and clustering-style similarity methods. Both are fragile under sparsity. Identifier joins fail when required keys are missing or inconsistent. Clustering can accommodate incomplete identifiers, but it introduces a different failure mode: similarity thresholds, distance metrics, and fuzzy grouping decisions that are difficult to govern and expensive to audit. These methods may work in narrow contexts, but they do not behave as infrastructure. They either break outright or produce results whose correctness is probabilistic and difficult to defend.

This case study proposes a multidisciplinary shift: applying graph theory—particularly concepts commonly used in social network analysis—to restore identity continuity under sparsity and heterogeneity. The central move is to replace "identity equals a single key" with "identity equals evidence-backed connectivity."

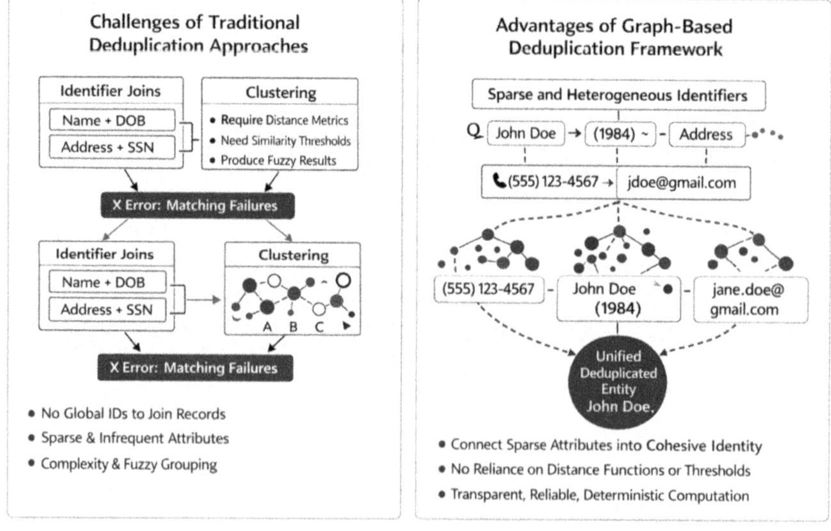

Fig. 5.5 Deduplication approaches: traditional versus graph-based

In this framework, the data grid is treated as a heterogeneous graph. Records and identifiers become vertices, and relationships become edges. Crucially, edges are not "friendships" or interactions as in social networks; they are redefined as identifying signals. A shared phone number, a reused email address, a historical address, or a cross-system reference becomes an explicit connective edge. Identity is then computed not by matching attributes directly, but by discovering connectivity structure—most notably, connected components. When multiple records are linked through explicit evidence paths, they are unified into the same component, and a stable enterprise entity identifier can be assigned to that component.

Figure 5.5 illustrates why this matters. On the right, sparse and heterogeneous identifiers that would fail under direct joins become connective bridges. A single attribute may be weak in isolation, but multiple weak signals can combine into a strong structural path. The graph does not require a perfect match on one global key; it integrates partial evidence into a coherent connectivity outcome. In this way, the system can "remember" an entity even when attributes evolve over time, because continuity is preserved through the network of evidence rather than through any single identifier.

The deeper innovation is infrastructural. Connectivity itself becomes a governed data product—a representational layer that echoes Chap. 4's System Representation methodology and "Everything as Data" philosophy. Instead of treating identity resolution as an ad hoc matching job, the grid materializes an explicit identity digital twin: a queryable structure showing why two records are unified, through which evidence paths, and under which deterministic rules. This yields an important property that many AI-driven deduplication systems lack: auditability. Unification is not justified by an opaque similarity score, but by a traceable path of evidence in the graph. This distinction also defines the boundary between deterministic and probabilistic approaches. Many AI-based deduplication systems rely on fuzzy inference, learned similarity functions, and confidence thresholds. Those methods can be powerful, but their outputs behave like black-box decisions unless heavily instrumented. In industrial environments where identity feeds compliance reporting, safety workflows, or operational decision systems, "mostly correct" is often insufficient. The graph-based framework offers a more infrastructure-grade alternative: deterministic connectivity rules, interpretable evidence chains, and controllable failure modes. Strategically, the outcome is the infrastructure of universal connectivity. The enterprise gains an identity memory that is not owned by any single source system schema. This strengthens the Canonical Modeling layer by ensuring that dimensions and facts can be anchored to stable entities even when upstream identifiers are fragmented. Downstream analytics and AI applications inherit a unified semantic foundation whose identity assignments are explainable and reproducible.

Taken together with the previous two case studies, this example reinforces the book's core argument: data modeling is not only schema design. It includes the explicit engineering of representational layers—transformation twins, governed AI boundaries, and connectivity-based identity—that make the Data Grid resilient under real-world complexity. The next chapter extends this principle from modeling into observability: how lineage and documentation form the nervous system that makes infrastructure behavior inspectable, diagnosable, and trustworthy at scale.

5.7 Further Reading

To extend the infrastructure-oriented data modeling doctrine developed in this chapter—particularly (i) lifecycle-bounded semantic responsibility (Bronze/Silver/Gold + volatility buffers), (ii) canonical modeling as an enterprise semantic backbone (grain, identity, temporal truth, composability), (iii) Transformation-as-Data as a logical digital twin of manufacturing logic, (iv) explicit white-box vs. black-box boundaries for AI augmentation, and (v) deterministic, graph-based entity unification under sparse and heterogeneous identifiers—the following resources provide complementary theoretical grounding and engineering patterns. These works collectively connect relational foundations, temporal and provenance formalisms, metadata-driven control, and graph/record-linkage methods relevant to infrastructure-grade modeling.

- Codd, E. F. (1970). "A Relational Model of Data for Large Shared Data Banks." Communications of the ACM.

    - Annotation: The foundational argument for declarative data representation and structural independence. While often cited for relational theory, its deeper relevance here is the infrastructure property of a shared semantic substrate: stable primitives, explicit structure, and predictable composition—core to the Canonical Modeling Layer's "semantic backbone" role.

- Kimball, R., & Ross, M. (2013). The Data Warehouse Toolkit (3rd ed.). Wiley.

    - Annotation: The most influential practical text on dimensional modeling and semantic consistency for analytics. It complements this chapter by clarifying grain definition, conformed dimensions, and fact design—especially useful when translating Gold-layer canonical entities into decision-oriented delivery models above the deterministic core.

- Inmon, W. H. (2005). Building the Data Warehouse (4th ed.). Wiley.

    - Annotation: A contrasting tradition emphasizing enterprise integration and subject-oriented modeling. Read alongside Kimball, it helps sharpen the chapter's argument that "enterprise truth" is an infrastructural asset—and that volatility must be isolated above the canonical backbone rather than injected into foundational layers. Snodgrass, R. T. (Ed.). (1995). The TSQL2 Temporal Query Language. Springer. Summary: A canonical reference for temporal data semantics and historical correctness. It supports the chapter's mandate that "temporal truth" must be explicit (history vs. current state) and reinforces why overwriting destroys auditability, back-testing, and causal analysis—especially in AI training and evaluation pipelines.

– Buneman, P., Khanna, S., & Tan, W.-C. (2001). "Why and Where: A Characterization of Data Provenance." ICDT.

  – Annotation: A clean conceptual foundation for provenance as a first-class property of data artifacts. It directly strengthens the chapter's emphasis on lineage and traceability as infrastructure, not documentation—particularly relevant when arguing that deterministic cores must remain auditable and reconstructable.

– Cheney, J., Chiticariu, L., & Tan, W.-C. (2009). "Provenance in Databases: Why, How, and Where." SIGMOD Record.

  – Annotation: A widely used survey that maps provenance models and their tradeoffs. It complements the Semantic Processing and System Representation perspectives by showing how lineage can be formalized—and why relying on inference from code/logs is brittle compared to declarative, queryable representations.

– Armbrust, M., et al. (2020). "Delta Lake: High-Performance ACID Table Storage over Cloud Object Stores." VLDB.

  – Annotation: A practical foundation for the chapter's Bronze/Silver determinism: ACID guarantees, transaction logs, and time travel enable replay, forensic reconstruction, and auditable evolution. It helps ground "deterministic origin" and "controlled change" in concrete storage/transaction mechanisms.

– Bhattacharya, I., & Getoor, L. (2007). "Collective Entity Resolution in Relational Data." ACM Transactions on Knowledge Discovery from Data.

  – Annotation: Establishes the idea that identity resolution can be improved by exploiting relational structure, not just attribute similarity. It bridges directly to the chapter's graph-based case study: identity emerges from connectivity and shared signals—an engineering move from "hard keys" to "structural evidence."

– Newman, M. E. J. (2018). Networks (2nd ed.). Oxford University Press.

  – Annotation: A rigorous, readable foundation for graph thinking (components, connectivity, community structure). It supports the chapter's reframing of deduplication as a network problem—where connected components become an interpretable, auditable mechanism for entity unification across sparse, heterogeneous identifiers.

– NIST. (2023). AI Risk Management Framework (AI RMF 1.0). National Institute of Standards and Technology.

  – Annotation: A governance-oriented framework that maps directly onto the chapter's AI boundary logic: traceability, accountability, and risk containment. It provides an external grounding for why AI outputs should be constrained to testable, reversible domains—with white-box control retained for structural invariants.

Collectively, these works reinforce Chap. 4's thesis: infrastructure-grade data modeling requires stable semantic primitives in the core, explicit handling of time and provenance, representable and governable manufacturing logic, bounded AI augmentation under deterministic control, and identity resolution methods whose correctness can be explained—not merely predicted.

Chapter 6
Data Lineage and Documentation

Abstract This chapter addresses system memory as a prerequisite for infrastructure transparency. It argues that lineage and documentation must be embedded within execution logic as structured, queryable metadata rather than maintained as external artifacts. The chapter examines the evolution from post hoc lineage reconstruction to runtime-captured, deterministic traceability. A case study illustrates how transformation rules represented as relational metadata enable impact analysis, dependency tracing, and governance enforcement. By formalizing lineage as an operational control mechanism, the chapter strengthens infrastructure observability and prepares the system for reliability engineering practices.

Keyword Deterministic traceability · Infrastructure observability ·
Machine-readable metadata · Operational provenance · Runtime lineage capture ·
Impact analysis

By the end of the previous chapter, we established a foundational principle: data modeling is not just about organizing tables or defining schemas. It is how organizations engineer trust properties into their data infrastructure. When modeling is done correctly, layered architectures transform raw operational signals into reusable enterprise knowledge. But structure alone does not create infrastructure-grade reliability. A system can be well-modeled and still fail the moment someone asks a simple question: where did this number actually come from?

If a system cannot explain how values were produced and used, it cannot operate as infrastructure-grade data systems are expected to. It is structured storage without operational provenance. Earlier generations of data platforms could tolerate this limitation. Pipelines were smaller, teams were localized, and failures were investigated manually. Institutional knowledge filled the gaps between design and reality. But modern data systems operate very differently. They function as distributed soft infrastructure powering real-time decision loops, machine learning pipelines, and increasingly, autonomous AI agents. In this environment, missing traceability is not a documentation inconvenience—it is an operational risk.

Z. T. Lee, *The Data Grid*, SpringerBriefs in Computer Science,
https://doi.org/10.1007/978-3-032-25004-9_6

Data lineage and modern documentation exist to close this gap. Lineage provides historical memory. Documentation provides semantic context. Together, they allow data systems to move from being externally observable to being internally explainable. In infrastructure-grade systems, this transition is increasingly required for safe automation, scalable AI adoption, and reliable cross-domain data reuse.

To bridge the gap between design intent and operational reality, this chapter concludes with a Case Study on Deterministic Lineage through Structured Logic Tables. We examine the practical advantage of treating transformation rules as queryable data rather than procedural code. By representing the "how" of data manufacturing as a live, structured document, we enable the infrastructure to expose lineage as queryable, near-real-time provenance. This ensures that lineage is no longer a secondary byproduct to be "inferred," but a primary, deterministic property of the soft infrastructure itself.

6.1   The Need for Memory in Data Infrastructure Systems

If you have worked on large data platforms long enough, you eventually encounter a class of failures that are not caused by infrastructure outages or schema changes, but by the inability to reconstruct history. Numbers change without obvious explanation. Downstream dashboards drift. Machine learning models degrade silently. Investigations become archaeology exercises rather than engineering workflows. These failures frequently point to the same root cause: the system has no reliable memory of how data was produced.

Data lineage addresses this by capturing the lifecycle of data across ingestion, transformation, and consumption of data as it moves through an infrastructure system—from source generation, through transformation layers, to final consumption. Historically, lineage was implemented as pipeline diagrams or table-level dependency graphs. While useful for visualization, these artifacts were never sufficient for operating complex data systems. Modern lineage must operate across multiple layers simultaneously. At the system level, lineage describes cross-platform data movement and domain-level dependencies. At the transformation level, lineage captures which logic version was applied and when. At the attribute level, lineage traces how individual columns were derived. At the most granular level, lineage captures record-level provenance, allowing the system to explain how a specific value was produced at a specific point in time.

This evolution is driven by a shift in how data is consumed: from human interpretation toward machine consumption. Traditional systems assumed human interpretation. Modern systems increasingly assume machine consumption. AI systems cannot infer context through institutional memory. Context must be explicitly encoded, machine-readable, and queryable.

Without lineage, AI systems operate on disconnected signals. With lineage, AI systems operate within a traceable decision framework. This difference becomes critical when AI outputs directly influence business operations, customer interactions, or regulatory reporting. In these environments, explainability is not merely a reporting feature—it becomes a safety requirement in high-stakes environments. Lineage therefore transforms data infrastructure from a data transport mechanism into a historical system of record for intelligence generation.

6.2 Making Lineage and Semantics Machine-Readable

Lineage alone is not sufficient if it exists only as visualization or logging. To support modern infrastructure use cases, lineage and documentation must be machine-readable and queryable.

Historically, documentation lived outside the system. It described system behavior but did not participate in execution. This model fails under scale because documentation inevitably diverges from implementation. In modern data infrastructure, documentation increasingly becomes executable metadata. The system does not read documentation. It executes it. Transformation logic, semantic definitions, governance rules, and pipeline dependencies are stored as structured data assets rather than external narrative text. This creates "living documentation": version-controlled, executable metadata that evolves with system logic.. Documentation evolves automatically as system logic evolves because documentation and execution share the same source of truth.

The convergence between lineage and machine-readable documentation creates a self-reinforcing feedback loop. When transformation logic changes, lineage updates automatically. When semantic definitions evolve, documentation updates automatically. When governance policies change, enforcement behavior updates automatically. The system becomes self-describing through metadata rather than external explanation. Semantic layers play a critical role in this architecture. Business definitions are encoded as structured objects rather than static documentation. This enables consistent metric computation, automated semantic propagation, and safe AI query interpretation. As data moves through the infrastructure, semantic context travels with it. Data becomes not only structurally consistent, but contextually self-describing.

Machine-readable lineage also enables impact simulation and more proactive system operation.. Instead of reacting to failures, organizations can simulate downstream impact before modifying transformation logic. Infrastructure maintenance can shift from reactive debugging toward more proactive, simulation-driven engineering.. Regulatory compliance becomes continuous rather than periodic. Data governance shifts from manual policy enforcement to automated metadata-driven control. From an economic perspective, machine-readable lineage enables measurement of data asset value. By tracking downstream usage, organizations can attribute business outcomes back to specific data assets. Data transitions from an intangible resource into a measurable infrastructure investment.

6.3 Embedding Lineage into the Execution Layer

The most important architectural shift in modern lineage systems is moving lineage capture from post-processing reconstruction into runtime execution. Modern data platforms implement lineage through centralized metadata control planes. These systems track schema evolution, transformation dependencies, execution history, data quality telemetry, and governance classification. Rather than reconstructing lineage after execution, modern systems capture lineage during execution itself.

Query parsers capture column derivation graphs. Transaction logs record transformation state transitions. Orchestration engines capture runtime dependency resolution. Version-controlled logic repositories capture transformation evolution across time. Together, these components produce deterministic, timestamped lineage aligned with actual system behavior. This shift is critical. Post-hoc lineage reconstruction is often incomplete.. Runtime lineage capture produces authoritative provenance. Embedding lineage into execution also enables higher-order infrastructure capabilities. Organizations can perform automated impact analysis before deploying logic changes. Systems can detect unused pipelines and eliminate redundant processing. Execution telemetry can identify performance bottlenecks and reliability risks.

However, building lineage into execution introduces engineering tradeoffs. High-resolution lineage can generate significant metadata volume. Not all data flows require record-level provenance. Many organizations adopt tiered lineage models, where high-risk data domains receive full lineage capture while lower-risk domains rely on aggregated lineage tracking. Implementation complexity is another major challenge. True end-to-end lineage requires integration across ingestion systems, transformation engines, orchestration frameworks, storage layers, and semantic platforms. Partial implementations create blind spots. Many organizations overestimate lineage completeness when only pipeline-level tracking exists. Organizational adoption also remains difficult. Many tcams implement lineage primarily for compliance rather than operational intelligence. Without cultural integration, lineage systems become passive reporting tools rather than active infrastructure components.

Perhaps the most subtle risk is false confidence. Lineage documents process history, not correctness. If transformation logic is flawed, lineage will faithfully document incorrect behavior. Lineage must therefore be paired with strong data quality engineering and reliability monitoring.

6.4 Lineage as a Foundation for Data System Reliability

As lineage systems mature, they push data infrastructure toward full observability. Systems become traceable, auditable, and introspective. The Data Grid transitions from a collection of hidden pipelines into a transparent intelligence system capable of explaining its own behavior. This transformation is essential for safe AI adoption.

When every data element carries transformation history and semantic context, intelligence generated by the system becomes reproducible and verifiable. But observability alone is not sufficient. A system can be fully observable and still produce unreliable outputs if the underlying data signal is degraded. Lineage explains where data came from and how it was processed, but it cannot ensure statistical stability, semantic consistency, or operational reliability. As data systems become more autonomous, this distinction becomes critical. Infrastructure must not only be explainable—it must be resilient. This realization represents the next stage of infrastructure maturity. Data integrity must be engineered continuously, not validated after the fact. Just as electrical grids rely on circuit breakers, monitoring systems, and predictive maintenance to ensure stable power delivery, modern data infrastructure must adopt reliability engineering principles to ensure only trustworthy signals propagate through the system.

In the next chapter, we move from observability to protection—from understanding the flow of intelligence to actively safeguarding it. If lineage and documentation provide the memory and language of the infrastructure, data quality and reliability provide its protection and containment mechanisms. Together, these layers ensure that the intelligence flowing through the Data Grid remains stable, trustworthy, and safe for autonomous decision-making.

6.5 Case Study: Deterministic Lineage Through Structured Logic Tables

The previous chapter established that data modeling is not complete without memory. A system may preserve grain, identity, and canonical semantics, yet still fail as infrastructure if it cannot explain how a value was produced. This case study operationalizes that principle by demonstrating how lineage becomes deterministic when transformation logic itself is represented as structured data.

From Inferred Lineage to Represented Lineage: In traditional environments, lineage is reconstructed after execution. SQL scripts are parsed, orchestration DAGs are scanned, and external metadata platforms attempt to infer dependency graphs. This process is inherently fragile. It introduces synchronization lag between execution and documentation, and it depends on code interpretation rather than declared structure. As soon as logic changes, lineage diagrams risk becoming stale. The result is a persistent metadata gap between what the system does and what the system can explain. Chapter 4 introduced the Transformation Logic Configuration Table as a digital twin of the data manufacturing process. When transformation rules are stored as structured relational metadata—rather than opaque procedural code—the gap between execution and explanation collapses. The logic that produces data becomes queryable data itself. Lineage ceases to be an inferred artifact and becomes a deterministic property of the infrastructure.

Lineage as a Relational Operation: Fig. 6.1 demonstrates this inversion. The query shown operates directly on the transform_logic_configuration table to retrieve the genealogy of a specific field (entity_key in entity_table). Because each transformation step is stored as a row—capturing source table, source column, target table, target column, and processing logic—lineage becomes a composable relational traversal. Instead of parsing nested SQL scripts, the system performs joins across metadata rows. Intermediate derivations are surfaced through self-joins, allowing the query to walk upstream dependencies step by step. The result is not a static diagram, but a live, executable lineage trace. Any engineer—or AI agent—with basic SQL access can retrieve the complete transformation history of a column in near real time. The significance is architectural. Lineage becomes SQL-native. It is no longer a visualization layer or external scanning service. It is an inherent capability of the data substrate itself.

The Living Document: Because transformation rules reside in a structured, version-controlled table, documentation and execution share a single source of truth. The configuration table functions as a living document. Unlike static Wiki pages or external documentation systems, it cannot drift independently from runtime behavior. When transformation logic changes, lineage changes automatically, because both are derived from the same metadata state. This structural symmetry eliminates interpretive ambiguity. The infrastructure does not attempt to describe its behavior retrospectively; it represents its behavior declaratively. In doing so, it aligns with the System Representation doctrine introduced in Chapter 4: infrastructure behavior must be formalized as a structured, queryable state.

Eliminating the Metadata Gap: The deeper innovation lies in collapsing the divide between execution and explanation. When lineage is represented as structured metadata: Semantics become machine-readable. AI systems can programmatically inspect upstream dependencies before consuming data, evaluating context and transformation reliability without relying on informal documentation. Impact analysis becomes deterministic. Before modifying a source table or transformation rule, engineers can execute an "impact query" to identify downstream fields, models, or metrics affected by the change. Governance becomes proactive. Instead of auditing after incidents occur, the system can simulate dependency impact prior to deployment.

This transforms lineage from a compliance artifact into an operational control mechanism. Infrastructure Memory as a First-Class Property. This case study demonstrates the practical consequence of the "Everything as Data" philosophy. When transformation logic is stored as structured metadata, the Data Grid acquires native memory. It remembers not only data values, but the exact structural path by which those values were produced. Lineage therefore becomes deterministic, queryable, and continuously synchronized with execution. The grid becomes self-describing. Its memory is no longer reconstructed through log archaeology; it is embedded in its representational fabric. In infrastructure terms, this is the difference between a system that can be observed and a system that can explain itself. By embedding lineage into the execution layer through structured logic tables, the Data Grid establishes the operational memory required for reliable automation, safe AI augmentation, and

```sql
SELECT
  1 AS step,
  d1.target_table,
  d1.target_column,
  d1.source_table,
  d1.source_column,
  d1.processing_logic
FROM
  transform_logic_configuration d1
WHERE
  d1.target_table = 'entity_table'
  AND d1.target_column = 'entity_key'
UNION ALL
-------- Intermediate Steps
SELECT
  9 AS step,
  d3.target_table,
  d3.target_column,
  d3.source_table,
  d3.source_column,
  d3.processing_logic
FROM
  transform_logic_configuration d1
    LEFT JOIN transform_logic_configuration d2
      ON d2.target_table = d1.source_table
      AND d2.target_column = d1.source_column
    LEFT JOIN transform_logic_configuration d3
      ON d3.target_table = d2.source_table
      AND d3.target_column = d2.source_column
WHERE
  d1.target_table = 'entity_table'
  AND d1.target_column = 'entity_key';
```

Fig. 6.1 Query to get data lineage—Demonstrates the practical application of the Transformation Logic Configuration Data Table for bloodline tracing. By executing a standard recursive SQL query against the structured metadata, the system can instantly retrieve the complete lineage of any given field (e.g., entity_key). This query-based approach replaces the need for proprietary third-party scanners or manual code parsing. It illustrates how the structured representation of logic allows both human engineers and AI agents to programmatically navigate the data's genealogy—identifying sources, intermediate steps, and transformation rules—directly within the data layer. This capability ensures that lineage is not only deterministic and always up-to-date but also natively accessible to anyone with basic SQL proficiency

scalable cross-domain reuse. Deterministic structure establishes trust. Deterministic memory preserves it.

6.6 Further Reading

To extend the observability, deterministic lineage, and self-describing infrastructure perspectives developed in this chapter—particularly the transition from post-hoc lineage reconstruction to runtime-embedded provenance, the formalization of transformation logic as queryable metadata, and the elevation of documentation into executable semantic state—the following academic and industry works provide complementary theoretical grounding and engineering practices. These resources focus on data provenance theory, metadata systems, observability architecture, impact analysis, and governance-aware automation.

- Buneman, P., Khanna, S., & Tan, W.-C. (2001). "Why and Where: A Characterization of Data Provenance." International Conference on Database Theory (ICDT).

  - Annotation: A foundational formalization of data provenance, distinguishing different types of dependency tracing (why-provenance, where-provenance). The paper provides theoretical grounding for treating lineage as a first-class, queryable property of data systems rather than an auxiliary visualization artifact. It supports the chapter's argument that provenance must be structurally representable, not inferred from code.

- Cheney, J., Chiticariu, L., & Tan, W.-C. (2009). "Provenance in Databases: Why, How, and Where." SIGMOD Record.

  - Annotation: A comprehensive survey of provenance models and implementation techniques. It clarifies the tradeoffs between logical inference, annotation-based tracking, and workflow reconstruction approaches. The survey reinforces the chapter's emphasis on deterministic lineage embedded within structured metadata rather than relying on heuristic or post-execution reconstruction.

- Davidson, S. B., & Freire, J. (2008). "Provenance and Scientific Workflows." ACM SIGMOD Record.

  - Annotation: Explores provenance capture in scientific workflow systems, emphasizing runtime tracking and reproducibility. The paper illustrates why lineage must be captured during execution rather than reconstructed afterward—a principle directly aligned with the chapter's advocacy for execution-layer embedded lineage.

- Halevy, A. Y., Rajaraman, A., & Ordille, J. (2006). "Data Integration: The Teenage Years." VLDB.

- Annotation: Discusses integration challenges in heterogeneous data environments, particularly dependency reasoning and schema mediation. The paper supports the argument that lineage must be cross-system and lifecycle-aware to remain meaningful at enterprise scale.

- Abadi, D. J., et al. (2016). "The Design of the Borealis Stream Processing Engine." CIDR.

  - Annotation: While focused on stream processing, this work highlights the importance of runtime metadata, execution tracking, and deterministic replay in distributed systems. It complements the chapter's position that lineage is most reliable when embedded directly in execution infrastructure.

- Armbrust, M., et al. (2020). "Delta Lake: High-Performance ACID Table Storage over Cloud Object Stores." VLDB.

  - Annotation: Demonstrates how transaction logs and time travel enable reproducibility and auditability. This aligns with the chapter's claim that infrastructure-grade lineage depends on deterministic state transitions recorded at runtime rather than inferred post hoc.

- Simmhan, Y. L., Plale, B., & Gannon, D. (2005). "A Survey of Data Provenance in e-Science." ACM SIGMOD Record.

  - Annotation: A broad survey examining provenance models across scientific domains. It highlights challenges of completeness, scalability, and metadata volume—directly relevant to the engineering tradeoffs discussed in the chapter regarding tiered lineage capture and metadata management.

- NIST. (2023). AI Risk Management Framework (AI RMF 1.0). National Institute of Standards and Technology.

  - Annotation: Establishes governance requirements for traceability, accountability, and explainability in AI-enabled systems. The framework reinforces the chapter's claim that lineage is not merely observability but a safety boundary for AI-driven automation.

- Kreps, J., Narkhede, N., & Rao, J. (2011). "Kafka: A Distributed Messaging System for Log Processing." NetDB.

  - Annotation: Introduces log-centric architectures where immutable event logs function as system memory. The log-as-source-of-truth paradigm complements the chapter's view of lineage as infrastructure memory embedded within execution flows.

- Fuller, A., Fan, Z., Day, C., & Barlow, C. (2020). "Digital Twin: Enabling Technologies, Challenges and Open Research." IEEE Access.

- Annotation: Reviews digital twin architectures emphasizing synchronization between state and representation. The chapter's structured-logic lineage model can be interpreted as a digital twin of transformation behavior, aligning provenance with real-time system state.

Collectively, these works reinforce the chapter's central thesis: lineage must evolve from static documentation and after-the-fact inference into deterministic, runtime-embedded infrastructure memory. When transformation logic, execution state, and provenance are unified within structured metadata, data systems become self-describing and audit-ready by design. In such architectures, explainability is not retrofitted—it is structurally guaranteed.

Chapter 7
Data Quality and Integrity

Abstract This chapter advances from traceability to reliability. It reframes data quality as a continuous engineering discipline and introduces measurable reliability contracts aligned with lifecycle boundaries. Quality enforcement is modeled as a system-level control function rather than episodic validation. The chapter defines yield metrics and threshold policies as operational indicators and presents a case study involving automated containment mechanisms that isolate unstable data flows. By integrating reliability engineering concepts into data infrastructure design, the chapter establishes protection mechanisms necessary for safe automation and AI augmentation.

Keyword Data Reliability Engineering (DRE) · Measurable reliability contracts · Data yield · Dynamic circuit breakers · Automated containment · Continuous engineering discipline

By the end of the previous chapter, we established that modern data infrastructure must be able to provide explainable, queryable provenance. Through lineage, executable metadata, and living documentation, data systems gain memory. They can reconstruct how data was produced, which transformations were applied, and how intelligence flows across organizational boundaries. This level of observability is a foundational requirement for operating data as infrastructure-grade systems.

However, observability alone does not guarantee correctness. A system can be fully traceable and still produce unreliable outcomes if the underlying data signal is degraded. A well-documented pipeline can still propagate biased distributions, broken joins, or semantically inconsistent logic. In high-automation environments, traceability without reliability often limits organizations to explaining failure after it occurs rather than preventing propagation. Modern data infrastructure therefore requires a second layer of engineering maturity. If lineage provides system memory, reliability engineering provides protection and containment mechanisms. This shift mirrors the evolution of many infrastructure domains. Early network systems focused

Z. T. Lee, *The Data Grid*, SpringerBriefs in Computer Science,
https://doi.org/10.1007/978-3-032-25004-9_7

on connectivity and routing visibility. Mature network systems introduced redundancy, fault isolation, and automated recovery. Data infrastructure is increasingly undergoing a similar transition.

In traditional data environments, data quality was often treated as downstream cleanup. Errors were detected after data reached reporting layers. This model was inefficient but survivable when decision speed was limited by human analysis cycles. In modern AI-driven environments, data flows continuously through automated decision loops, optimization systems, and model training pipelines. When unreliable data enters these systems, failures propagate quickly and often invisibly. In this environment, data quality is no longer primarily about report correctness in many AI-driven environments. It is about decision safety under automated and high-velocity execution. Data integrity becomes a core infrastructure property, similar to availability or latency in distributed systems. This shift introduces Data Reliability Engineering (DRE), a discipline that treats data quality as a measurable, enforceable system metric rather than a post-processing validation activity. At its core, DRE answers a simple operational question: can this data be trusted to drive automated decisions?

To illustrate how DRE principles are operationalized within the soft infrastructure, this chapter concludes with a Case Study on Automated Quality Contracts and Dynamic Circuit Breakers. We move beyond passive monitoring to explore how quality thresholds can be defined as structured, executable data. By integrating these "quality contracts" directly into the orchestration loop, the infrastructure can automatically halt or downgrade data flows that fail to meet reliability standards. This transforms data integrity from a manual validation task into an automated, protection-oriented infrastructure behavior.

7.1 From Quality Checks to Reliability Engineering

Traditional data quality systems operate like monitoring dashboards. They detect anomalies, generate alerts, and rely on human intervention. In high-throughput automated environments, this model is insufficient. By the time humans investigate anomalies, unreliable data may already have influenced downstream models and operational decisions.

Reliability-oriented data systems embed protection directly into data movement and transformation. Instead of logging failures, they enforce reliability thresholds during execution. When reliability contracts are violated, data propagation can be interrupted, isolated, or downgraded in trust classification based on executable contracts. This represents an operational shift in enforcement strategy. Traditional systems optimize for data completeness. Reliability-oriented systems optimize for decision correctness. In automated environments, partially incorrect data can be more harmful than missing data in automated decision loops because it produces highly confident but incorrect automated behavior.

In practice, reliability enforcement spans three core dimensions. Structural reliability ensures schema integrity, data type stability, and required field completeness.

Statistical reliability ensures that data distributions behave within expected ranges across time. Semantic reliability ensures logical consistency across business entities and transformation logic. Reliability enforcement must also operate during execution, not after it. When reliability checks are embedded into transformation logic and orchestration workflows, data integrity becomes more enforceable and observable within defined execution boundaries. Over time, reliability signals accumulate into historical system knowledge, allowing infrastructure to detect instability patterns and reduce the likelihood of downstream failures.

7.2 Measuring Data Reliability as an Operational Metric

A key principle of DRE is that data quality must be measurable using operational metrics, not just validation rules. Modern data infrastructure benefits from continuous reliability indicators similar to error budgets and availability targets used in distributed systems.

One useful analogy comes from industrial manufacturing yield. In manufacturing, yield measures the percentage of produced components that meet production standards. Data systems increasingly apply similar thinking through the concept of data yield—the proportion of collected data that is safe for downstream intelligence workloads such as model training, analytics, or automated decision systems. Not all data is equally valuable. Data with severe missingness, sampling bias, or structural inconsistency can reduce model performance and increase decision risk. Reliability-oriented systems therefore measure and optimize usable data yield rather than total data volume. Another critical metric dimension involves data maintenance cycles. Physical infrastructure components degrade over time and require periodic recalibration. Data systems experience similar degradation through concept drift, schema evolution, and behavioral changes in upstream systems. DRE supports periodic revalidation of data assets against statistical baselines and semantic contracts. This ensures that data maintains predictive value and operational reliability over time.

Data lifecycle economics also becomes a reliability consideration. Not all data retains long-term value. Low-quality or obsolete data increases storage cost, governance overhead, and security exposure. DRE introduces lifecycle optimization where data retention decisions consider downstream dependency value, operational risk, and expected future utility. In this model, data retirement becomes an engineering and economic decision rather than a storage cleanup activity.

7.3 How Reliability Engineering Manifests in Real Data Systems

In production systems, DRE manifests through embedded reliability enforcement, automated fault isolation, and automation-assisted remediation workflows.

Reliability enforcement begins at ingestion boundaries. Structural validation ensures that data entering the system meets minimum schema and format guarantees. Statistical monitoring evaluates whether incoming data aligns with historical distribution baselines. Semantic enforcement validates cross-entity logical constraints. These checks are not passive. They are executed as part of data movement and transformation logic.

Fault isolation mechanisms prevent unreliable data from contaminating downstream intelligence layers. Instead of failing entire pipelines, modern systems isolate unreliable partitions, quarantine suspect records, and allow healthy data flows to continue. This mirrors fault isolation design in distributed infrastructure systems. Self-healing data workflows leverage lineage, execution telemetry, and historical reliability signals to identify recurring upstream instability patterns. Over time, data infrastructure can shift from reactive debugging toward more proactive, telemetry-driven maintenance. Instead of discovering data failures after dashboards break, systems identify instability trends before they affect decision layers.

Reliability signals also enable system-level optimization. By analyzing reliability topology across transformation graphs, organizations can identify fragile dependencies, redundant data products, and unused pipeline outputs. This transforms data infrastructure from passive storage into an actively optimized intelligence distribution system.

7.4 Cross-Disciplinary Foundations of Data Reliability Engineering

Data Reliability Engineering draws heavily from established reliability disciplines across engineering domains. Industrial manufacturing contributes to yield optimization thinking. Instead of maximizing production volume, mature systems optimize usable output quality. This directly maps to usable data yield optimization.

Infrastructure maintenance engineering contributes lifecycle recalibration models. Just as electrical transformers require periodic inspection, data assets require periodic statistical and semantic recalibration to maintain predictive accuracy. Economic engineering contributes to lifecycle cost modeling. Data storage and governance are not free. Data assets must be evaluated based on long-term business value, risk exposure, and downstream dependency criticality. Site Reliability Engineering contributes automated failure detection and isolation design. Modern data systems increasingly apply SRE principles such as automated rollback, fault containment zones, and reliability budget management. AI safety engineering contributes risk-weighted data acceptance strategies. Training and inference systems require higher reliability thresholds than exploratory analytics environments. DRE enables differentiated reliability enforcement based on downstream risk level.

7.5 The Role of DRE in AI-Native Infrastructure Operations

AI systems fundamentally change data reliability requirements. Traditional analytics workflows tolerate moderate noise because humans interpret results. Automated AI systems do not have this safety layer. When AI models are trained or executed on unreliable data, they produce confident but incorrect outputs. Lineage enables AI explainability. Reliability engineering enables AI trustworthiness. Without reliability enforcement, explainability becomes post-incident storytelling rather than pre-incident prevention. In AI-native infrastructure, data reliability must be treated as part of model safety. Training datasets must meet reliability contracts. Feature pipelines must maintain statistical stability. Inference systems must detect real-time data drift. DRE provides the operational framework required to enforce these guarantees.

7.6 Building the Integrity Layer of the Data Grid

The transition from data quality management to data reliability engineering represents a major milestone in data infrastructure maturity. Data systems evolve from passive data processing environments into actively protected intelligence infrastructure.

When reliability enforcement becomes embedded in execution logic, data infrastructure becomes safer under enforceable reliability boundaries.. Instead of relying on downstream detection, the system prevents unreliable signals from entering high-trust decision layers. This shift also enables long-term infrastructure optimization. Reliability metrics provide objective signals for pipeline prioritization, data lifecycle decisions, and upstream system remediation investments. Data moves from a passive asset toward an actively managed infrastructure resource.

However, reliability engineering alone is not sufficient. Reliability protects signal integrity, but it does not guarantee business correctness or adaptive intelligence. As data systems continue to automate decision processes, infrastructure must evolve beyond reliability toward continuous quality optimization and adaptive signal interpretation. In the next chapter, we extend this foundation by examining how quality enforcement, anomaly detection, and adaptive monitoring systems form the continuous protection layer of modern data infrastructure. If lineage provides the memory of the system and reliability engineering provides its safety mechanisms, data quality engineering becomes the continuous protection layer— continuously monitoring, enforcing, and containing integrity risks across data flows.

7.7 Case Study

7.7.1 Layer-Aware Quality Contracts as Additive Semantic Tags

In conventional platforms, quality is often implemented as passive monitoring: checks run after pipelines, and alerts are produced when anomalies are detected. This model fails under automation. Invalid or degraded data can reach canonical layers and power dashboards, features, and decision systems before a human can intervene. From the semantic elevation perspective, the core issue is that quality meaning is not encoded in the data artifact. A dataset may be "available" but not "trustworthy," and downstream systems cannot distinguish the two deterministically.

As Figs. 7.1 and 7.2 show, this case study introduces layer-aware quality contracts whose outcomes are recorded as structured tags—so that each lifecycle stage appends its own "semantic headers," analogous to protocol headers in the OSI stack. These tags do not replace data; they wrap data with inspectable reliability state. Quality rules should not be hard-coded into individual pipelines. Instead, they are stored in a Quality Contract Table aligned to lifecycle layers. The daemon (or execution controller) reads transformation rules and quality contracts together, executes validations, and writes results back as execution metadata. Quality becomes a living, queryable subsystem of the grid. A contract only becomes "infrastructure" when its enforcement leaves a durable state. The grid therefore writes quality results into a Quality Execution Log, producing structured tags that downstream systems can query.

```sql
-- Quality contracts are declared as structured metadata.
CREATE TABLE IF NOT EXISTS quality_contracts (
    layer STRING, -- bronze | silver | gold | platinum | app
    target_table STRING,
    target_column STRING, -- nullable for table-level checks
    check_type STRING, -- not_null | uniqueness | freshness | range | regex | distribution
    threshold_value STRING, -- generic storage: '0.99', 'P1D', '[-3,3]', etc.
    severity STRING, -- warn | quarantine | stop
    action_on_failure STRING, -- warn | stop | downgrade | quarantine
    contract_version STRING,
    is_active BOOLEAN,
    updated_at TIMESTAMP
) USING DELTA;
```

Fig. 7.1 Quality contract table

```
-- Bronze (fidelity): ensure ingestion headers exist and ingestion is complete enough.
INSERT INTO quality_contracts VALUES
('bronze', 'bronze_entity_raw', 'source_event_id', 'not_null', '1.0', 'stop', 'stop', 'v1', true, current_timestamp()),
('bronze', 'bronze_entity_raw', 'ingested_at',     'not_null', '1.0', 'stop', 'stop', 'v1', true, current_timestamp());

-- Silver (engineering validity): standardization and reconciliation signals.
INSERT INTO quality_contracts VALUES
('silver', 'silver_entity', 'entity_id',    'not_null',   '1.0', 'stop', 'stop', 'v1', true, current_timestamp()),
('silver', 'silver_entity', 'entity_id',    'uniqueness', '1.0', 'stop', 'stop', 'v1', true, current_timestamp()),
('silver', 'silver_entity', 'processed_at', 'freshness',  'PT6H', 'warn', 'warn', 'v1', true, current_timestamp());

-- Gold (semantic backbone): canonical integrity constraints.
INSERT INTO quality_contracts VALUES
('gold', 'dim_entity', 'entity_sk', 'not_null',   '1.0', 'stop', 'stop', 'v1', true, current_timestamp()),
('gold', 'fact_event', 'event_id',  'uniqueness', '1.0', 'stop', 'stop', 'v1', true, current_timestamp());
```

Fig. 7.2 Definition of contracts

7.7.2 *Dynamic Circuit Breakers and the Determinism Gradient*

Semantic elevation renders quality visible; reliability engineering renders quality enforceable. The architectural shift is therefore from passive detection to active containment. If degraded data is merely flagged but still allowed to propagate into canonical layers, lineage may later explain what occurred—but explanation does not prevent damage. Infrastructure must not only observe degradation; it must constrain it. This case study introduces dynamic circuit breakers as a control mechanism embedded within the lifecycle architecture. When the measured data yield falls below a declared contract threshold, the execution controller triggers a containment action that restricts propagation across lifecycle boundaries. In doing so, it protects the Deterministic Structural Core from semantic contamination. Circuit breakers operate at layer boundaries, not within ad hoc pipeline code. The lifecycle segmentation of the Data Grid provides natural containment lines. Bronze, Silver, and Gold collectively form the structural backbone; if trust degrades at Silver, upward flow into Gold must be conditionally gated. When the validation query for a required release state returns no qualifying rows, the Gold materialization step is deterministically blocked—or rerouted into a downgrade or quarantine path. This guarantees that semantic trust in canonical layers is never constructed on unstable technical foundations.

For such containment to function under automation, circuit breakers require a measurable control variable. Binary pass/fail checks are insufficient in high-volume systems. Yield—the proportion of records meeting declared quality contracts—provides an engineering-grade reliability signal. It quantifies how much usable data is safely available and enables graded control decisions rather than blunt halts. As illustrated in Figs. 7.3 and 7.4, yield transforms quality from a static validation result into a continuous operational metric suitable for deterministic governance.

```
-- Identify failing checks that require propagation control.
WITH failing AS (
  SELECT *
  FROM quality_execution_log
  WHERE run_id = 'run_2026_02_24_001'
    AND status = 'fail'
    AND action_taken IN ('stop', 'downgrade', 'quarantine')
)
SELECT
  layer,
  target_table,
  COLLECT_SET(action_taken) AS required_actions,
  COUNT(*) AS failing_checks
FROM failing
GROUP BY layer, target_table;
```

Fig. 7.3 Determine breaker decisions from the log

```
CREATE TABLE IF NOT EXISTS table_release_status (
  run_id          STRING,
  layer           STRING,
  table_name      STRING,
  release_status  STRING,    -- released | blocked | downgraded | quarantined
  reason          STRING,
  decided_at      TIMESTAMP
) USING DELTA;
```

Fig. 7.4 "Release status" for each table per run

7.8 Further Reading

To extend the reliability, quality-contract, and circuit-breaker perspectives developed in this chapter—particularly the treatment of data quality as executable metadata, the alignment of validation rules with lifecycle boundaries, the use of yield as an engineering control variable, and the containment of degraded signals through deterministic enforcement—the following works provide complementary theoretical grounding. These references span reliability engineering, control theory, data validation systems, and automated governance in distributed infrastructures.

- Sculley, D., et al. (2015). "Hidden Technical Debt in Machine Learning Systems." Advances in Neural Information Processing Systems (NeurIPS).

  - Annotation: A seminal paper describing how silent data quality degradation propagates systemic risk in automated systems. It reinforces the chapter's claim that passive monitoring is insufficient in AI-augmented environments and that infrastructure must contain low-trust signals before they influence downstream decision systems.

– Laprie, J.-C. (1992). "Dependability: Basic Concepts and Terminology." Springer.

  – Annotation: A foundational text in reliability engineering defining fault, error, failure, and containment boundaries. The distinction between detection and containment directly informs the circuit-breaker model introduced in this chapter, where degraded data is treated as a controllable fault condition within the lifecycle architecture.

– Leveson, N. (2011). Engineering a Safer World: Systems Thinking Applied to Safety. MIT Press.

  – Annotation: Introduces system-theoretic accident models emphasizing control structures over component inspection. The book's emphasis on enforced constraints rather than post-hoc analysis parallels the transition from passive quality alerts to active lifecycle gating in data infrastructure.

– Hellerstein, J. L., Zhang, Y., & Shahabuddin, P. (2004). Feedback Control of Computing Systems. Wiley.

  – Annotation: A practical guide to applying control theory in distributed systems. The concept of measurable control variables (analogous to Data Yield) and feedback loops supports the chapter's argument that automated containment requires quantitative reliability signals rather than binary checks.

– Rahman, M., & Kayes, A. (2022). "Explainable Artificial Intelligence for Cyber-Physical Systems." ACM Computing Surveys.

  – Annotation: Discusses bounded autonomy and verifiable AI integration in controlled environments. It reinforces the necessity of deterministic enforcement layers when probabilistic systems operate on real-time data signals.

– Simmhan, Y. L., Plale, B., & Gannon, D. (2005). "A Survey of Data Provenance in e-Science." ACM SIGMOD Record.

  – Annotation: Reviews provenance systems in scientific workflows and highlights scalability challenges in fine-grained tracking. It complements this chapter by clarifying how runtime metadata capture enables reproducibility but must be paired with validation and containment to ensure signal integrity.

– Armbrust, M., et al. (2020). "Delta Lake: High-Performance ACID Table Storage over Cloud Object Stores." VLDB.

  – Annotation: Demonstrates how transaction logs and time-travel capabilities enable deterministic replay and enforcement. These mechanisms support the integrity layer described in this chapter by ensuring that quality decisions and containment actions are version-controlled and reproducible.

- NIST. (2023). AI Risk Management Framework (AI RMF 1.0). National Institute of Standards and Technology.

  - Annotation: Establishes governance principles for trustworthy AI, including traceability, risk containment, and impact assessment. The framework aligns directly with the chapter's doctrine that degraded data must be prevented from propagating into high-stakes automated systems.

Collectively, these works reinforce the chapter's central thesis: quality in infrastructure-grade data systems must be engineered as enforceable control, not merely monitored as diagnostic output. When validation rules are structured as metadata, yield becomes a measurable control signal, and lifecycle boundaries act as containment lines, the Data Grid evolves from an observable system into a protected one. In such architectures, trust is not inferred after failure—it is maintained through deterministic enforcement.

Chapter 8
Data Governance and Security

Abstract This chapter integrates governance and security into the infrastructure core. It formalizes policy enforcement as structured, executable metadata applied across the data lifecycle. The chapter adopts a zero-trust perspective and demonstrates how access control, masking, and compliance policies can be modeled as deterministic contracts. A case study illustrates how relational policy representation enables continuous auditability and measurable enforcement. By embedding governance within system architecture, the chapter completes the trust foundation required for scalable and regulated AI systems.

Keyword Zero-trust data architecture · Security-as-a-Contract · Metadata-driven enforcement · Quantitative risk engineering · Deterministic trust foundation · Continuous auditability

In the previous chapter, we established that modern data infrastructure must enforce reliability. Reliable data ensures that signals are structurally valid, statistically stable, and semantically consistent. However, reliability alone does not guarantee safe outcomes. Data can be technically correct and still be misused, exposed, or applied in ways that create regulatory, ethical, or economic risk. Modern data infrastructure therefore requires an enforceable trust control layer. If reliability ensures data is safe for computation, governance and security ensure data is safe for authorized and compliant use.

In traditional systems, governance and security were typically implemented as external policy overlays. Access reviews, audit reports, and periodic compliance checks attempted to enforce safe behavior after systems were already in operation. In modern AI-driven environments, this model is insufficient. Data moves continuously across system boundaries, and automated decision systems consume data without human mediation. Governance and security must therefore become embedded enforcement mechanisms within system execution paths.

Modern infrastructure shifts from perimeter-based security to identity-driven trust enforcement. Instead of securing physical network boundaries, systems verify identity, intent, and usage context continuously. No user, application, or AI agent should

Z. T. Lee, *The Data Grid*, SpringerBriefs in Computer Science,
https://doi.org/10.1007/978-3-032-25004-9_8

be trusted by default under Zero-Trust principles. Data interactions should be evaluated in real time wherever risk classification requires it. This model reflects the broader industry shift toward Zero-Trust architectures across distributed systems. Security and governance must also operate across the full data lifecycle. At ingestion boundaries, systems verify source authenticity and detect early-stage contamination risks. During transformation, sensitive attributes are masked, tokenized, or encrypted. At consumption layers, data usage must remain traceable, auditable, and aligned with regulatory and ethical requirements. This helps ensure data systems remain safe even as automation increases.

To illustrate the transition from abstract policies to automated enforcement, this chapter concludes with a Case Study on Security as a Queryable Contract Layer. We explore how representing access rights and masking rules as structured metadata allows security to become a native, metadata-driven property of the data infrastructure. By treating security policies as "data," we enable the execution control layers to dynamically apply protection policies—such as real-time masking or tokenization—based on the consumer's context. This transforms governance into a high-speed, programmable control plane that enables Zero-Trust enforcement down to the individual record level where required.

8.1 Treating Data Risk as an Engineering and Economic Problem

One of the most important evolutions in modern governance is the shift from qualitative compliance thinking to quantitative risk engineering. Governance decisions increasingly require economic justification, not just regulatory alignment. Data failures produce measurable financial consequences. Breaches create regulatory penalties, legal exposure, operational downtime, and loss of customer trust. As organizations scale AI-driven decision systems, these risks can compound across automated decision systems. A single data governance failure can propagate across automated systems if not isolated early.

Engineering economic decision frameworks provide a structured way to evaluate governance investments. Data risks can be modeled using probability-weighted loss scenarios. Security controls can be prioritized based on expected risk reduction per unit cost. This allows organizations to move from uniform security enforcement toward risk-optimized protection strategies.

This approach reflects principles widely used in reliability engineering, safety engineering, and infrastructure planning. Instead of assuming all risks are equal, organizations allocate protection resources based on economic impact and failure probability. In practice, this means critical data domains, high-risk regulatory datasets, and AI training pipelines receive stronger protection controls than low-risk analytical data. This perspective also changes how organizations think about data assets. Data is not only a source of value. It is also a potential liability. Governance must therefore balance data utility, storage cost, compliance exposure, and long-term risk accumulation.

8.2 Governance and Security in AI-Native Systems

AI-driven infrastructure introduces new classes of threats that do not exist in traditional data environments.

Data poisoning attacks target data itself rather than infrastructure. Attackers inject biased or adversarial records that appear structurally valid but influence model behavior. These attacks will be difficult to detect using traditional rule-based validation because poisoned data often looks statistically normal at small scales. Prompt injection attacks target AI reasoning layers. Attackers craft inputs designed to bypass safety constraints and induce models to reveal restricted data or execute unintended actions. In these cases, the attack surface is not network infrastructure but semantic interpretation.

These risks require expanding security thinking beyond traditional access control and encryption. Modern systems must validate data intent, input behavior, and model interaction patterns. Governance and security must extend into the semantic layer of AI interactions. Dynamic data protection becomes critical in this environment. Instead of static data masking, modern systems adjust data exposure dynamically based on identity, risk classification, and usage context. The same dataset may present different views depending on the consuming system's authorization level. This allows organizations to maintain full data fidelity internally while minimizing exposure risk externally.

AI systems also increase the importance of traceability and accountability. Organizations must be able to explain why automated decisions were made, which data influenced those decisions, and whether that data was authorized for use. Governance therefore becomes deeply connected to lineage and reliability engineering introduced in earlier chapters.

8.3 Building the Trust Layer of Modern Data Infrastructure

Governance and security represent a critical control layer required to operate data as infrastructure. If lineage provides system memory and reliability engineering provides signal safety, governance provides trust enforcement. Together, these layers allow organizations to build data systems that are explainable, reliable, and safe to operate at scale. Governance transitions from compliance overhead into an infrastructure capability that enables safe automation, faster regulatory adaptation, and higher-confidence AI deployment.

As data systems continue to evolve, governance must also become adaptive and intelligence-driven. Future systems will increasingly automate compliance monitoring, risk detection, and usage enforcement as part of core infrastructure behavior. In the next chapter, we shift focus from protection toward optimization and execution. We examine how modern data pipelines evolve from static workflow systems into adaptive intelligence distribution networks capable of dynamically routing, transforming, and optimizing data movement across the entire infrastructure stack.

8.4   Case Study: Security as a Queryable Contract Layer

In many organizations, data security is still implemented as an external wrapper: perimeter controls, static roles, and periodic audits that sit outside the data itself. This approach was workable when platforms were small and access paths were limited. It becomes brittle as modern data infrastructure evolves into distributed soft infrastructure—serving self-service analytics, cross-domain reuse, and increasingly, AI agents operating through automated workflows. In that environment, the central governance problem is no longer "who is inside the network," but what a given actor may access, under which conditions, and with what transformation constraints. This case study proposes a structural shift consistent with the Data Grid doctrine: treat security not as an external configuration, but as an internal, machine-readable contract layer. Access rights, masking rules, and sensitivity classifications are represented as structured metadata tables within the grid. Security becomes a queryable policy—a native property of data transactions rather than a static perimeter assumption (Fig. 8.1).

This change matters for three reasons. First, it eliminates policy drift: the rule being enforced is the rule being stored. Second, it enables deterministic propagation: when policy changes, downstream behavior changes immediately, without requiring every pipeline to be rewritten. Third, it makes risk measurable. When policy

```
CREATE TABLE IF NOT EXISTS security_policy (
  agent_id        STRING,     -- user / service principal / AI agent
  purpose         STRING,     -- analytics | ml_training | support | etc.
  table_name      STRING,
  column_name     STRING,
  permission      STRING,     -- ALLOW | DENY
  mask_policy     STRING,     -- NONE | REDACT | HASH | TOKENIZE
  sensitivity     STRING,     -- PUBLIC | INTERNAL | CONFIDENTIAL | PII
  policy_version  STRING,
  is_active       BOOLEAN,
  updated_at      TIMESTAMP
) USING DELTA;
```

Fig. 8.1 Contract table: security policy metadata

```sql
INSERT INTO security_policy VALUES
-- Analyst: can access customer_id; can access PII only through masking
('analyst_001', 'analytics', 'gold_customer', 'customer_id', 'ALLOW', 'NONE',   'INTERNAL', 'v1', true, current_timestamp()),
('analyst_001', 'analytics', 'gold_customer', 'email',       'ALLOW', 'HASH',   'PII',      'v1', true, current_timestamp()),
('analyst_001', 'analytics', 'gold_customer', 'phone',       'ALLOW', 'REDACT', 'PII',      'v1', true, current_timestamp()),

-- Support: can see phone (redacted); email is denied
('support_007', 'support',   'gold_customer', 'customer_id', 'ALLOW', 'NONE',   'INTERNAL', 'v1', true, current_timestamp()),
('support_007', 'support',   'gold_customer', 'phone',       'ALLOW', 'REDACT', 'PII',      'v1', true, current_timestamp()),
('support_007', 'support',   'gold_customer', 'email',       'DENY',  'NONE',   'PII',      'v1', true, current_timestamp());
```

Fig. 8.2 Example policy inserts (illustrative, not exhaustive)

is data, exposure is also data. Governance shifts from qualitative statements ("PII is protected") to quantitative observability ("which columns are exposed to which agents, and under what masking regime"). At a practical level, this is an application of the System Representation methodology from Chap. 4. The grid is no longer asked to "interpret" scattered security logic across tools. Instead, the grid represents security intent as a structured state and enforces it as part of normal execution and query behavior. The outcome is an infrastructure-grade trust layer: fast, auditable, and automation-compatible (Fig. 8.2).

8.5 Further Reading

To expand on governance and security as an embedded trust control layer in modern data infrastructure—Zero-Trust identity-driven enforcement across the lifecycle, quantitative risk engineering/economic modeling of data exposure/liability, AI-specific threats (poisoning, prompt injection, semantic risks), dynamic protection (context-based masking/tokenization), and security policies as queryable/metadata-driven contracts for deterministic, auditable enforcement—the following resources provide targeted frameworks, patterns, and case studies on adaptive, data-centric trust mechanisms in AI-native environments.

1. NIST. (2025). Zero Trust Architecture for Data-Centric Security (SP 800-207A update).https://csrc.nist.gov/publications/detail/sp/800-207a/final

   a. Annotation: Extends Zero Trust to data-level enforcement (identity + context + intent verification), emphasizing continuous evaluation and dynamic policy application—aligning with the shift from perimeter to embedded trust and lifecycle coverage.

2. Gartner. (2025). Data Security Posture Management: Risk Quantification and Economic Prioritization.https://www.gartner.com/en/documents/4023456

   a. Annotation: Introduces quantitative risk scoring (probability × impact) for data assets, economic justification of controls, and treating data as liability—directly supporting the chapter's engineering/economic framing and risk-optimized protection strategies.

3. OWASP. (2025). AI Security and Privacy Guide: Data Poisoning and Prompt Injection Defenses.https://owasp.org/www-project-ai-security-and-privacy-guide

   a. Annotation: Details defenses against poisoning (input validation, provenance checks) and prompt injection (semantic-layer guards, context-aware restrictions)—relevant to AI-native threats and need for governance extending into semantic/execution layers.

4. IBM. (2025). Dynamic Data Masking and Tokenization in AI Pipelines.https://www.ibm.com/topics/dynamic-data-masking

   a. Annotation: Explains runtime, context-based masking/tokenization based on user intent/risk—mirroring the case study's dynamic protection during transmission and policy-driven exposure adjustment.

5. Collibra. (2025). Policy-as-Code and Metadata-Driven Governance for Zero Trust.https://www.collibra.com/blog/policy-as-code-zero-trust

   a. Annotation: Covers representing governance/security rules as structured metadata for automated enforcement and auditability—aligning with security as queryable contract layer and deterministic propagation of policy changes.

6. Imperva. (2025). Data-Centric Security: Queryable Policies and Real-Time Enforcement.https://www.imperva.com/blog/data-centric-security-policies

   a. Annotation: Discusses storing access/masking rules as queryable entities for runtime application and exposure calculation—supporting the case study's Security Policy Metadata Table and quantifiable "Total Potential Exposure."

7. Microsoft. (2025). Purview Data Governance: AI Risk and Compliance in Automated Systems.https://learn.microsoft.com/en-us/purview/ai-risk-governance

   a. Annotation: Frames governance for AI traceability/accountability (data usage provenance, regulatory alignment)—relevant to AI-driven accountability and balancing utility with risk in automated decision loops.

8. Forrester. (2025). Economic Models for Data Governance Investments.https://www.forrester.com/report/economic-models-data-governance

   a. Annotation: Provides frameworks for probability-weighted loss scenarios and ROI prioritization of controls—echoing the chapter's treatment of risk as quantitative/economic problem and data as potential liability.

9. Adversa AI. (2025). Defending Against Data Poisoning in Enterprise Pipelines.https://adversa.ai/blog/data-poisoning-defenses

   a. Annotation: Explores detection/isolation of poisoned inputs in training/ inference flows—supporting expanded security thinking for AI-specific threats and semantic-layer validation.

10. OneTrust. (2025). Metadata-Driven Access and Masking for AI-Native Data Flows.https://www.onetrust.com/blog/metadata-driven-access-ai

   a. Annotation: Details metadata tables for context-aware access/masking/ tokenization—practical extension of the case study on policy-as-data for high-speed, programmable trust enforcement.

Chapter 9
Data Orchestration

Abstract This chapter redefines orchestration as a declarative control plane rather than a collection of workflow scripts. It proposes a configuration-driven execution model in which routing logic, scheduling rules, and dependencies are expressed as structured metadata. A persistent reconciliation mechanism ensures alignment between declared state and runtime behavior. The chapter demonstrates how such an approach improves observability, resilience, and deterministic activation. By elevating orchestration to an infrastructure subsystem, it enables stable automation under distributed conditions.

Keyword Declarative control plane · Pipeline-as-Data · State-driven execution · System daemon abstraction · Continuous reconciliation · Deterministic activation

In earlier generations of data systems, pipelines were primarily designed to move data from one location to another. Reliability and performance were measured in terms of throughput, latency, and job completion success. In modern AI-driven data infrastructure, this definition is no longer sufficient. Pipelines do not simply move data. They shape how intelligence is generated, distributed, and consumed across the organization.

If previous chapters established memory (lineage), safety (reliability), and trust (governance), pipelines represent the operational coordination layer of the infrastructure. They determine how quickly data products and derived intelligence can be delivered, where processing occurs, and how system load is distributed across the data platform. Traditional pipeline architectures treat pipelines as code—Python scripts, workflow DAGs, or orchestration logic embedded in platform-specific tools. While powerful, this model introduces operational friction. Pipeline logic becomes separated from the data it operates on. Infrastructure behavior becomes dependent on specialized software engineering knowledge. As organizations scale data and AI workloads, this separation can become a significant operational bottleneck.

Modern infrastructure requires a shift from treating pipelines as software artifacts to treating them as data assets. This is the foundation of the "Pipeline as Data" philosophy. Instead of describing pipeline behavior through imperative scripts, pipeline

Z. T. Lee, *The Data Grid*, SpringerBriefs in Computer Science,
https://doi.org/10.1007/978-3-032-25004-9_9

intent is expressed through declarative metadata stored directly in the data platform. The pipeline definition becomes queryable, versionable, and analyzable like any other data asset. This shift aligns with the broader evolution of infrastructure systems across engineering domains. Mature infrastructure systems replace manual control logic with standardized, data-driven control planes. In data systems, this control plane is implemented through structured pipeline metadata models.

To bridge the gap between declarative intent and physical execution, this chapter concludes with a Case Study on Orchestration as a System Daemon. We explore how the transition to "Pipeline as Data" enables a centralized control plane where long-running orchestration daemons—rather than manual triggers—continuously evaluate the state of the grid. By monitoring metadata signatures and data-readiness signals, these daemons activate infrastructure execution workflows ensuring that intelligence flows across the grid with the same predictable and reproducible reliability characteristics as a biological nervous system or an automated power grid.

9.1 Building Pipeline Infrastructure as a Data-Native Control Plane

The core architectural pattern behind Pipeline as Data is the separation of control intent from execution mechanics. Instead of embedding pipeline logic in orchestration tools, pipeline behavior is defined through structured configuration tables that act as routing and execution control maps.

In this model, each pipeline is defined as a row in a standardized metadata structure. Source location, destination target, transformation logic reference, execution frequency, dependency relationships, and reliability policies are all stored as data rather than code. Deploying a new pipeline can often be reduced to inserting or updating a configuration record. Execution is handled by long-running daemon services that continuously evaluate pipeline state. Instead of scheduling jobs based purely on time triggers, execution decisions are made based on data readiness state. When upstream dependencies reach a valid state, downstream transformations can be triggered automatically.. This state-centric execution model aligns pipeline behavior directly with data lifecycle state rather than tool-specific scheduling semantics.

This architecture also reduces tool lock-in. Because pipeline behavior is defined through platform-neutral metadata, execution engines can change without rewriting pipeline logic. The control plane remains stable even as compute engines evolve from batch processing frameworks to streaming engines or cloud-native SQL execution environments. Pipeline metadata also enables infrastructure introspection. Because pipeline definitions are stored as data, they can be analyzed for dependency risk, performance bottlenecks, and unused processing paths. This transforms pipeline orchestration from manual workflow management into an optimizable infrastructure system.

9.2 Extending Pipelines to the Edge: Distributed Intelligence and Pre-Processing

As data generation moves closer to real-world sensors, applications, and user interactions, centralized processing models can become increasingly inefficient.. This is where distributed processing and edge intelligence, as explored in edge AI research, become critical extensions of modern pipeline design. In traditional centralized architectures, all raw data is transmitted into the core data platform before filtering or transformation occurs. As data volume grows, this model creates unnecessary network pressure and increases processing latency. Modern infrastructure increasingly shifts filtering and preprocessing logic toward the edge of the data generation environment.

Edge filtering acts as an intelligent pre-processing layer. Instead of transmitting all raw data, edge systems apply early-stage validation, anomaly detection, and compression logic before forwarding data to core infrastructure layers. This is similar to how smart meters perform local aggregation and filtering before transmitting usage data to centralized grid control systems. In more advanced implementations, lightweight AI models can operate directly at the data generation edge. These models perform early classification, noise reduction, or signal extraction before data enters the central pipeline. This reduces core infrastructure load while improving signal quality entering downstream AI training and analytics systems.

This distributed pipeline model aligns with broader distributed systems design patterns. Processing occurs closer to data origin when possible, while centralized systems focus on high-level aggregation, cross-domain modeling, and long-term storage. This reduces network cost, improves system responsiveness, and increases overall infrastructure scalability. Edge-aware pipeline design also improves system resilience. When edge systems can perform partial processing locally, core infrastructure outages have reduced impact on data generation continuity.

9.3 Pipeline Virtualization as an Infrastructure Abstraction Layer

When pipelines are treated as data and execution becomes state-driven, data infrastructure gains a new level of operational flexibility. Pipelines can be created, modified, or retired through metadata updates rather than code deployments. AI systems can participate in infrastructure optimization by analyzing pipeline behavior and suggesting structural improvements.

This architecture also enables self-documenting infrastructure. Pipeline metadata simultaneously acts as execution logic, documentation, and governance control surface. This reduces the traditional gap between system design and system implementation. From an organizational perspective, pipeline virtualization lowers the barrier to infrastructure participation. Data scientists, analytics engineers, and even automated AI agents can define pipeline behavior using declarative data interfaces rather than software development environments. As infrastructure becomes more automated, pipeline systems transition from static workflow engines into adaptive intelligence distribution networks capable of optimizing data movement dynamically based on system load, data priority, and downstream demand.

9.4 Enabling Frictionless Intelligence Flow Through Infrastructure Orchestration

The evolution from pipeline-as-code to pipeline-as-data represents a major step toward fully automated data infrastructure. By embedding pipeline logic into data-native control planes and extending processing toward the edge, organizations can build infrastructure where data movement is governed by standardized, observable, and optimizable system logic.

In this model, data engineers shift from implementing individual workflows to designing infrastructure rules for how data should move across the system. Pipelines become part of the infrastructure fabric rather than external automation scripts. With movement, reliability, and governance now integrated into the infrastructure layer, the final stage of modern data architecture focuses on how intelligence is consumed. In the next chapter, we examine how data consumption systems evolve from static reporting layers into adaptive intelligence interfaces that power real-time decision systems, AI agents, and autonomous enterprise workflows.

9.5 Case Study: The Daemon as a Data-Native Control Plane

A recurring failure mode in data platforms is not the absence of orchestration, but the misplacement of orchestration. Execution intent is scattered across scripts, scheduler interfaces, YAML files, and tool-specific DAG definitions. Even when "pipeline-as-code" is achieved, orchestration remains a static declaration that depends on external triggers, human coordination, or fragile tool semantics to become real. The system can describe what should happen, but it cannot reliably operate itself as a continuous infrastructure organism. The result is an activation gap. However, by the time we reach this chapter, the Data Grid has already undergone a structural transformation. Through the Digital Twin methodology introduced earlier, transformation logic, quality contracts, security policies, and execution intent have all been represented as structured metadata tables. The infrastructure no longer hides its behavior in opaque scripts; it stores its operational state as queryable data. What remains unresolved is not representation—but activation. Once orchestration intent exists as a structured state, the engineering question becomes: how do we continuously reconcile that declared state with runtime execution?

To answer this, we deliberately migrate a methodological abstraction from operating systems: the daemon process. This is not a superficial analogy but a structural transfer of control philosophy. In operating system design, a daemon is not a one-time task runner. It is a persistent background service that continuously enforces desired system conditions—monitoring state, coordinating work, handling retries, logging outcomes, and remaining alive across time. It exists not to execute a single instruction, but to maintain systemic stability through ongoing reconciliation.

When applied to the Data Grid, the daemon becomes the activating mechanism of the Digital Twin. The metadata tables describe the desired orchestration state; the daemon continuously reads that state and reconciles it with the physical execution plane. In this way, static table structures are no longer passive documentation—they become operational control inputs. Figure 9.1 provides the conceptual anchor. A Linux daemon runs continuously in the background, interacting with the operating system and external services while maintaining a stable execution loop. The defining property is persistence. The daemon does not wait for a human to "run it." It remains active, waking cyclically, evaluating conditions, and enforcing system policy. By importing this abstraction into data infrastructure, orchestration transitions from episodic workflow execution to continuous state maintenance. The system no longer merely runs pipelines; it maintains alignment between declared intent and actual state. Figure 9.2 makes this operational. The loop is a control-cycle:

- Wake/Trigger (initial or cyclic): the daemon exits sleep and begins a reconciliation cycle.
- Read configuration state: it reads the orchestration configuration tables (and any related quality/security contracts) to determine the system's desired state.

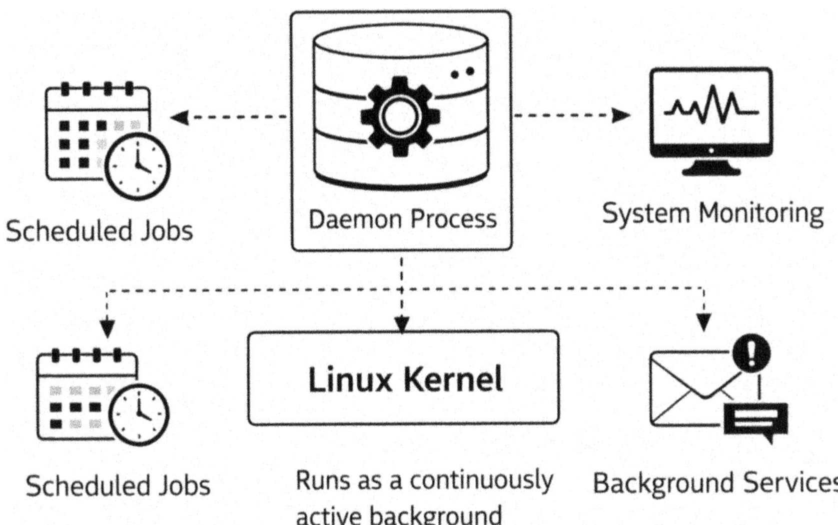

Fig. 9.1 Linux daemon process

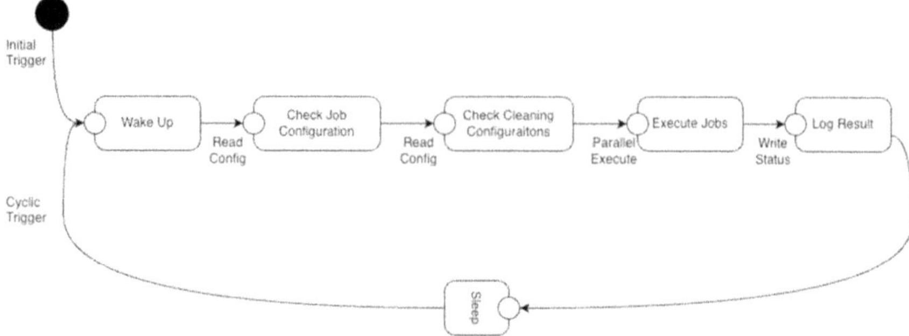

Fig. 9.2 Daemon Execution Loop—Continuous reconciliation cycle of the data-native control plane. The loop is activated either by an initial signal or a scheduled wake event, transitioning the daemon from an idle state into evaluation mode. Upon activation, the daemon reads orchestration and housekeeping configurations from structured metadata tables to determine the system's declared desired state. It then evaluates eligibility conditions and dispatches qualified transformation jobs for parallel execution, converting declarative orchestration intent into concrete runtime actions. After execution, the daemon records outcomes—run status, timestamps, and execution telemetry—into history tables before returning to a sleep state. This closed-loop pattern establishes orchestration as a persistent, configuration-driven control mechanism rather than an episodic workflow trigger

- Evaluate eligibility: it checks which jobs are due, enabled, safe, and valid under current constraints.
- Parallel execute: it dispatches eligible transformations to the execution plane.
- Write status / log results: it records outcomes—run history, success/failure states, timestamps, and reasons.
- Return to sleep: it yields control until the next wake cycle.

This is the crucial shift: orchestration is no longer "a set of procedures that run." It becomes a deterministic control loop that repeatedly reconciles the system's actual state against its declared intent. That framing is directly consistent with the System Representation and Control view from Chapter 4: control is achieved through structured intent + divergence detection + reconciliation + telemetry.

Figure 9.3 shows what the daemon reads: a job_orchestration_configuration table that stores orchestration intent as a queryable state. The significance is not the individual columns; it is the architectural contract they represent.

- job_name/target definition expresses what should be produced (often aligned to a target table or modeled artifact).
- schedule_cron + timezone expresses when the system should attempt reconciliation for that target.
- trigger_mode distinguishes between continuous scheduled control and explicit human intervention.
- adhoc_request_id/adhoc_run_at makes one-time execution intent first-class— captured inside the same data substrate rather than via external tooling.

```sql
%sql
CREATE TABLE job_orchestration_configuration (
    job STRING COMMENT 'job name, which is the target table name. Example: dim_member',
    enabled_flag INT COMMENT '1=enabled, 0=disabled. If disabled, daemon will skip.',
    timezone STRING
    | COMMENT 'Timezone used to evaluate schedule_cron_5 for scheduled runs. Example: America/Chicago.',
    schedule_cron_5 STRING
      COMMENT '5-field cron in the given timezone. Current daemon supports fixed daily pattern: "m h * * *" (e.g., "0 5 * * *").',
    trigger_mode STRING
      COMMENT 'Execution mode. SCHEDULED=normal cron-based runs. ADHOC=one-time run request managed by daemon.',
    adhoc_request_id STRING
      COMMENT 'One-time adhoc request key (idempotency key). Daemon runs ADHOC only if trigger_mode=ADHOC and this is NOT NULL/empty.',
    adhoc_requested_at TIMESTAMP COMMENT 'When the adhoc request was created (audit).',
    adhoc_run_at TIMESTAMP
      COMMENT 'Optional. If NULL => ASAP (next daemon tick). If NOT NULL => daemon will run only when now_utc >= adhoc_run_at (treated as UTC timestamp).',
    created_at TIMESTAMP COMMENT 'Row created timestamp (audit).',
    updated_at TIMESTAMP COMMENT 'Row last updated timestamp (audit).'
) USING DELTA
COMMENT 'Daemon schedule table for config-driven loads. Supports normal scheduled runs and one-time adhoc reruns.';
```

Fig. 9.3 Job Orchestration Configuration Data Table—Physical schema of the metadata-driven orchestration control surface. This table formalizes execution intent as structured, queryable state rather than embedded procedural logic. Core attributes—such as job_name (target definition), schedule_cron (recurring schedule alignment), and trigger_mode (automated vs. manual activation)—encode the lifecycle semantics of orchestration directly within the data layer. The inclusion of adhoc_request_id and adhoc_run_at elevates one-time execution intent to a first-class, data-native construct. By centralizing orchestration parameters in a structured SQL representation, the table provides a deterministic contract that the Daemon continuously reconciles and enforces—converting orchestration from tool-bound workflow logic into a governed, state-driven control plane

- enable_flag is the simplest but most powerful mechanism: turning orchestration into a governable state toggle rather than a code change.

The result is a "data-native control plane." Instead of hiding execution semantics in tool-specific artifacts, the platform expresses orchestration as structured metadata, readable and enforceable by the daemon in a deterministic way. In practical terms, this collapses a large category of operational work into ordinary data operations: inserting a request row, toggling a flag, or updating a schedule becomes sufficient to change system behavior—because the daemon continuously interprets and enforces that state.

9.6 Further Reading

To extend the operating-system and distributed control-plane perspective developed in this case study—particularly the migration of the daemon abstraction into data infrastructure, the reconciliation of desired versus actual state, and the treatment of orchestration as a persistent control loop—the following works provide foundational and complementary grounding.

- Tanenbaum, A. S., & Bos, H. (2015). Modern Operating Systems (4th ed.). Pearson.

    - Annotation: A comprehensive treatment of operating system design, including process models, daemons, scheduling, and background services. The discussion of long-lived system services and state management directly informs the adaptation of the daemon abstraction as a continuous control component within data infrastructure.

– Hellerstein, J. L., Zhang, Y., & Shahabuddin, P. (2004). Feedback Control of Computing Systems. Wiley.

  – Annotation: Introduces control-theoretic principles for computing systems, including feedback loops, stability, and reconciliation of desired and observed states. This text provides theoretical grounding for viewing the daemon execution loop as a control system rather than a simple scheduler.

– Burns, B., Grant, B., Oppenheimer, D., Brewer, E., & Wilkes, J. (2016). "Borg, Omega, and Kubernetes." Communications of the ACM.

  – Annotation: Describes large-scale cluster orchestration systems built around declarative desired-state reconciliation. The concept of controllers continuously aligning actual state with declared configuration closely parallels the data-native control plane described in this chapter.

– Kleppmann, M. (2017). Designing Data-Intensive Applications. O'Reilly Media.

  – Annotation: Explores distributed systems design, consistency models, logs, and state transitions. The book's treatment of durable state, idempotent operations, and failure recovery complements the deterministic orchestration model presented here.

– Bass, L., Clements, P., & Kazman, R. (2021). Software Architecture in Practice (4th ed.). Addison-Wesley.

  – Annotation: Discusses architectural tactics for modifiability, availability, and separation of concerns. Its emphasis on explicit architectural control layers supports the structural separation between metadata-defined orchestration intent and execution mechanisms.

Collectively, these works reinforce the chapter's central claim: orchestration matures into infrastructure when execution intent is expressed as a structured state and continuously reconciled by a persistent control process. By migrating the daemon abstraction from operating systems into the Data Grid, orchestration becomes not a tool-bound workflow, but a governed, state-driven subsystem capable of deterministic activation and resilient automation.

Chapter 10
Data Consumption

Abstract This chapter examines the transition from infrastructure capability to decision capability. It analyzes how structured metadata and lifecycle discipline enable governed, reproducible data access across analytical and AI-driven interfaces. A case study demonstrates controlled natural-language interaction with infrastructure through metadata mediation, ensuring auditability and boundary enforcement. The chapter concludes by positioning consumption as a formally engineered interface between infrastructure and intelligent applications.

Keyword Decision capability · Semantic metadata mediation · Natural language orchestration · Closed-loop decision systems · Agent-ready infrastructure · Metadata-driven transparency

In the previous chapters, we focused on building the foundation of modern data infrastructure. We established how data systems gain memory through lineage and documentation, how they maintain safety through reliability engineering, how they enforce trust through governance and security, and how they enable reliable delivery of data products and derived intelligence through data-driven pipeline orchestration. Together, these layers transform data platforms from collections of tools into infrastructure systems capable of operating at scale.

However, infrastructure alone does not directly create business value. Infrastructure creates potential. Value is realized only when intelligence is consumed and applied to real decisions. Historically, data consumption was treated as the final step of the data lifecycle. Data was processed, stored, modeled, and then exposed through dashboards and reports. In modern AI-driven organizations, consumption is no longer the end of the pipeline. It is an active, continuous interaction layer between data infrastructure and business execution systems.

This chapter focuses on how modern organizations convert infrastructure capability into decision capability. If earlier chapters focused on building a stable and trustworthy data grid, this chapter focuses on how that grid powers real business intelligence and operational automation. The shift is not simply from data storage to data access. The shift is from data reporting to decision systems.

Z. T. Lee, *The Data Grid*, SpringerBriefs in Computer Science,
https://doi.org/10.1007/978-3-032-25004-9_10

To bridge the final gap between complex infrastructure and human intent, this chapter concludes with a Case Study on Natural Language Orchestration via Semantic Metadata. We explore how a meticulously labeled and semantically rich Data Grid transforms the consumption experience. By providing AI systems with structured contextual metadata, the grid enables users to query and orchestrate data through natural language alone. This shift can significantly reduce the need for manual coding at the consumption layer, turning the Data Grid into an AI-compatible operational system that translates business conversation directly into actionable intelligence.

10.1 From Dashboards to Intelligent Interfaces

For the past two decades, dashboards have been the dominant interface for data consumption. Dashboards made complex systems observable. They standardized metrics, centralized reporting, and created shared operational visibility across organizations.

However, dashboards were built for a human-driven decision model. Data teams defined metrics, analysts built visualizations, and business users consumed predefined outputs. This model works well when business questions are predictable and decision cycles are slow. It breaks down when decision speed increases and business questions become more dynamic. Dashboards operate using a passive information push model. Data teams decide what insights should be surfaced, and users consume those outputs. This creates a structural limitation. Dashboards can show what happened, but they rarely explain why it happened or what should happen next. When deeper analysis is required, users must request additional development work. This introduces latency between insight and action. Modern data consumption systems are shifting toward interactive and intelligent interfaces. Large language models and AI agents introduce a new interaction model where users communicate with data systems through natural language. Instead of navigating dashboards, users express intent, and systems can translate that intent into executable data logic in near real time.

In this model, data access becomes conversational rather than navigational. Users no longer search for dashboards. Data systems can respond directly to business questions. This reduces decision latency and allows organizations to operate closer to real-time intelligence.

10.2 Building Reliable AI-Driven Data Consumption

For AI-driven consumption to be reliable, it must be built on top of strong data infrastructure layers. AI interfaces cannot operate safely on raw or loosely defined data. They require stable semantic definitions, reliable transformation pipelines, and enforced governance controls.

The semantic layer becomes the primary interface between AI systems and enterprise data. Instead of allowing AI models to construct logic dynamically, semantic models define official business vocabulary, entity relationships, and metric definitions. This ensures that AI-generated insights remain aligned with organizational truth. This approach can significantly reduce hallucination risk. When AI systems operate against semantic models, they retrieve validated definitions rather than attempting to infer business logic dynamically. Business questions map directly to pre-defined metric logic rather than dynamically generated transformation queries.

Modern AI consumption systems also enable proactive intelligence delivery. Instead of waiting for users to ask questions, AI-assisted systems can monitor business signals and generate recommendations. These systems can detect anomalies, evaluate potential business impact, and suggest potential actions based on historical patterns and predictive models. Another major shift is personalization. Traditional dashboards deliver identical views to all users. AI-driven systems adapt insight delivery based on role, context, and historical behavior. Each user effectively gains access to a personalized data assistant capable of filtering and prioritizing relevant intelligence automatically.

10.3 From Insight Generation to Closed-Loop Decision Systems

The most important evolution in modern data consumption is the transition from insight generation to closed-loop execution. Traditional data systems generated reports, and humans translated those reports into actions. Modern systems increasingly connect data insights directly to operational workflows.

Closed-loop data systems connect observation, analysis, and execution into a continuous feedback cycle. When anomalies are detected, systems can evaluate downstream impact and, where appropriate, trigger automated response workflows. For example, supply chain systems can automatically reroute shipments based on predicted delays, or pricing systems can adjust recommendations based on real-time cost signals. This transition changes how organizations measure data platform value. Instead of measuring dashboard adoption or report usage, organizations measure decision velocity and decision accuracy. The true value of data infrastructure appears in how quickly and correctly organizations respond to real-world events.

Closed-loop systems also reduce cognitive load on human operators. Instead of monitoring dashboards continuously, teams focus on exception handling and strategic oversight. Routine operational adjustments are handled automatically by infrastructure-level intelligence systems.

The evolution of data consumption reflects a broader shift in how organizations interact with intelligence systems. In early data environments, value was created by making information visible. In modern environments, value is created by making intelligence actionable. When data consumption is integrated directly into operational systems, intelligence becomes continuously available within operational workflows. Users do not need to search for insights. Insights appear automatically when and where they are needed. Decision support becomes part of daily workflows rather than a separate analytical process. This shift also represents the final stage of modern data infrastructure maturity. Infrastructure is no longer defined by how data is stored or processed. It is defined by how effectively intelligence can be delivered and applied. Across this book, we have described the transformation of data from a static resource into a dynamic infrastructure system. We defined data as a standardized utility, built layered architectures for reliability and trust, automated data movement through metadata-driven pipelines, and enabled intelligent consumption through AI-driven interfaces.

In the next chapter, we expand this vision further by examining how intelligent systems integrate directly into business workflows. We move beyond consumption and into utilization, exploring how AI-driven applications turn infrastructure intelligence into continuous operational optimization.

10.4 Case Study: Natural Language Orchestration via Semantic Metadata

Throughout this book, we have progressively shifted data infrastructure away from procedural scripts and toward structured, queryable state. Transformation logic is stored as metadata. Quality contracts are represented as executable thresholds. Security policies are expressed as structured governance records. Orchestration intent is encoded in configuration tables and activated by a persistent daemon. By the time we reach the domain of data consumption, the grid is no longer a collection of pipelines—it is a semantically labeled control system.

The next transformation is therefore not structural but cognitive. Historically, interacting with data systems required fluency in technical languages. Business intent had to be translated into SQL queries, Python scripts, or scheduler configurations before the system could respond. This translation layer introduced friction, dependency on specialized engineers, and increased the likelihood of misalignment between intent and implementation. The limitation was not computational power, but interface design.

When the Data Grid is richly structured—when tables declare explicit grain, columns carry descriptive semantics, contracts define constraints, and transformation logic is stored as relational records—the infrastructure becomes inherently interpretable. It is readable not only by engineers, but by Large Language Models. The metadata layer functions as a machine-readable semantic map of the system's behavior.

Figure 10.1 illustrates this architectural shift. An AI Agent acts as the cognitive bridge between human natural language and the structured control plane. A user does not write code. Instead, they express intent conversationally: "Add a new column,"

"Adjust the filter," "Rerun this job," or "Exclude inactive users from the Silver layer." The agent interprets this request against the metadata tables that already define transformation logic, execution schedules, and lifecycle boundaries. Rather than generating opaque procedural code, the agent proposes deterministic updates to structured configuration records. The daemon, introduced in the previous chapter, remains the enforcement authority. It reconciles the declared desired state against runtime conditions and activates execution accordingly. This design preserves the core doctrine of the Data Grid: determinism remains intact. The AI does not bypass infrastructure safeguards, nor does it introduce uncontrolled scripts into the execution plane. It interacts exclusively with the metadata control layer, which is versioned, auditable, and governed. In doing so, the system collapses the historical translation gap between business intent and technical implementation. Natural language becomes a high-level programming interface—not because code disappears, but because code has already been transformed into structured data.

The innovation here is not conversational querying alone. It is the alignment of human cognition with a deterministic control substrate. Low-friction interaction does not compromise structural integrity because the AI is constrained to operate within the same metadata fabric that governs orchestration, quality, and security. Domain

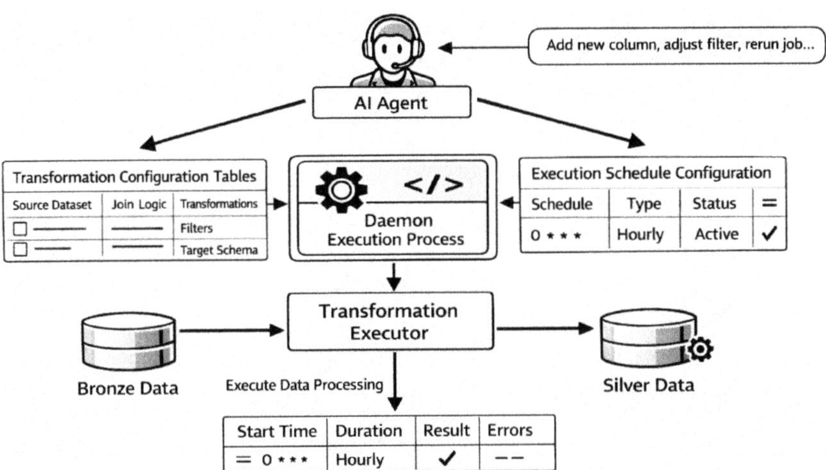

Fig. 10.1 Natural Language Interaction with the Metadata Control Plane—illustrates the architectural flow where an AI Agent serves as the cognitive bridge between human natural language and physical data execution. By leveraging semantically rich metadata—such as descriptive table and column names—the agent can interpret business intent and translate it directly into system actions. Instead of requiring users to write complex SQL or Python code, the AI Agent interacts directly with structured Transformation Configuration Tables and Execution Schedules. For instance, a user can simply request to "exclude inactive users," and the agent identifies the relevant metadata to perform a precise update on the logic table. This ensures that the data orchestration remains deterministic and structured, empowering non-technical domain experts to manage data flows through simple conversation while eliminating the friction of manual code-centric interfacing

experts can participate directly in managing data flows without manipulating procedural artifacts, and the system remains resilient because every change flows through a structured, enforceable state model. In this sense, the Data Grid becomes agent-ready. It is not merely compatible with AI; it is designed for safe cognitive augmentation. Natural language serves as the entry point, structured metadata serves as the control surface, and the daemon enforces execution under deterministic constraints. Data consumption thus evolves from code-centric interaction to semantically governed dialogue—without sacrificing reliability, traceability, or governance discipline.

10.5 Further Reading

To extend the human–computer interaction and agent-ready infrastructure perspectives developed in this case study—particularly the treatment of metadata as a machine-readable semantic map, the use of natural language as a controlled interface, and the preservation of deterministic execution under AI mediation—the following works provide complementary theoretical and practical grounding.

- Shneiderman, B. (2022). Human-Centered AI. Oxford University Press.

    - Annotation: Argues for AI systems that augment rather than replace human decision-making. The book emphasizes controllability, transparency, and structured interfaces—principles aligned with constraining AI interaction to metadata-driven control planes rather than opaque execution paths.

- Norman, D. (2013). The Design of Everyday Things (Revised ed.). Basic Books.

    - Annotation: A foundational work on interface design and cognitive ergonomics. Norman's emphasis on affordances, visibility, and feedback loops reinforces the importance of semantically labeled metadata as a readable interface between human intent and system behavior.

- Guha, R. V., Brickley, D., & Macbeth, S. (2016). "Schema.org: Evolution of Structured Data on the Web." Communications of the ACM.

    - Annotation: Discusses how structured metadata enables machine interpretation at scale. The paper supports the argument that richly labeled data structures are prerequisites for reliable machine reasoning and agent-based interaction.

- Zaharia, M., et al. (2018). "Accelerating the Machine Learning Lifecycle with MLflow." IEEE Data Engineering Bulletin.

    - Annotation: Describes metadata-driven tracking and model lifecycle management. It illustrates how structured metadata layers enable automation and reproducibility, paralleling the deterministic control surface required for safe AI-assisted orchestration.

- Burns, B., Beda, J., & Hightower, K. (2019). Kubernetes: Up & Running (2nd ed.). O'Reilly Media.

  - Annotation: Explains declarative infrastructure where desired state is expressed as structured configuration and reconciled by controllers. This mirrors the pattern in which AI proposes state changes while enforcement remains within a deterministic control loop.

- Amershi, S., et al. (2019). "Guidelines for Human-AI Interaction." CHI Conference on Human Factors in Computing Systems.

  - Annotation: Provides design principles for systems in which humans and AI collaborate. The emphasis on predictable behavior, user control, and system transparency aligns directly with the metadata-mediated natural language interface described in this chapter.

Collectively, these works reinforce the chapter's core thesis: natural language can serve as a viable programming interface only when infrastructure behavior is already expressed as a structured, governed state. When semantic metadata becomes the control surface, AI interaction enhances usability without eroding determinism.

Chapter 11
The Data Grid—A Forward-Looking Synthesis

Abstract The final chapter synthesizes the architectural framework into a coherent infrastructure doctrine. It integrates lifecycle segmentation, semantic transparency, system representation, and bounded AI augmentation into a unified model for AI-era data infrastructure. The chapter discusses implications for organizational design, interoperability, and long-term system evolution. It concludes that durable intelligence requires disciplined, observable, and continuously operating soft infrastructure, and positions the Data Grid as a formal engineering blueprint for achieving that objective.

Keyword Data Grid Synthesis · Infrastructure Doctrine · Deterministic Structural Core (DSC) · Engineering Blueprint · Durable Intelligence · Soft Infrastructure Maturity

In the opening pages of this book, we began with a historical observation: major industrial transformations do not endure because of technological breakthroughs alone. They endure because infrastructure matures. Mechanization scaled only after production systems were standardized. Electrification reshaped society only once generation and transmission grids stabilized energy delivery. The digital revolution became global only when layered communication protocols were built upon reliable electrical and computational foundations. In every case, technology accelerated change, but infrastructure sustained it. The AI era follows the same structural law.

Machine learning models, generative systems, and autonomous agents dominate attention. Yet their long-term viability depends not on model size or algorithmic novelty, but on the reliability and governability of the systems that feed, regulate, and constrain them. Intelligence does not operate in abstraction. It consumes structured signals, depends on semantic continuity, and propagates decisions across organizational processes. If the substrate beneath it is unstable, opaque, or semantically inconsistent, intelligence amplifies disorder rather than value.

This is the central claim of this book: data must be reclassified. It is no longer sufficient to treat data as a strategic asset, a byproduct of applications, or fuel for analytics. In AI-native environments, data functions as soft infrastructure. It is a

Z. T. Lee, *The Data Grid*, SpringerBriefs in Computer Science,
https://doi.org/10.1007/978-3-032-25004-9_11

continuously operating substrate through which intelligence is generated, distributed, validated, and operationalized. The name we have given to this substrate is the Data Grid. The Data Grid is not a product framework. It is not a technology stack. It is not a competitive architecture pattern alongside lakehouses, data mesh, or data fabric. It is an engineering doctrine. Its purpose is to formalize the structural conditions under which data systems become infrastructure-grade: reliable, observable, reproducible, and evolution-ready.

Throughout this work, four methodological dimensions have formed the backbone of that doctrine.

The first is lifecycle discipline. Data infrastructure must be segmented horizontally across responsibility boundaries—generation, stabilization, canonical modeling, domain composition, and intelligent consumption. These layers are not convenience abstractions. They are structural containment zones. Ingestion Consistency preserves source-fidelity and replayability. Engineering Validity enforces technical interoperability and structural normalization. Canonical Modeling establishes reusable semantic backbones insulated from volatility. Above these layers, business composition and application intelligence introduce flexibility without contaminating structural invariants. Together, the lower lifecycle layers constitute what we defined as the Deterministic Structural Core. Within this core, reproducibility must be guaranteed. Above it, controlled specialization may occur. This creates a determinism gradient that allows innovation without systemic fragility.

The second dimension is semantic elevation. Infrastructure maturity requires not only that data flows through layers, but that it remembers how it moved. Rather than destructively transforming records, each stage should append structured state: validation results, rule identifiers, transformation lineage, quality indicators, governance classifications. Meaning accumulates additively. Data becomes progressively self-describing. In this model, governance is not retrofitted documentation; it is an embedded state. Lineage is not reconstructed from logs; it is carried by the artifacts themselves. Semantic elevation ensures that abstraction does not erase transparency.

The third dimension is system representation. Traditional data environments remain procedural ecosystems. Pipelines execute scripts. Orchestration triggers jobs. Monitoring emits logs. Such systems function, but they remain opaque. Infrastructure-grade systems must represent their own operational behavior as structured state. Transformation intent, dependency topology, quality policies, access contracts, and execution telemetry must be formalized declaratively and version-controlled. When control logic converges with data assets into a unified metadata fabric, the infrastructure becomes introspectable. Primary systems—structured data tables—are regulated by explicitly represented secondary systems—governance, quality, orchestration, and observability layers. The platform achieves recursive self-representation. It becomes a digital twin of its own operation.

The fourth dimension is explicit AI boundary engineering. The defining tension of the intelligence era is the coexistence of probabilistic inference and deterministic infrastructure. AI systems are capable of generating code, synthesizing transformations, and optimizing workflows. Yet infrastructure must remain auditable, controllable, and reversible. The critical engineering question is not whether AI should be applied, but where its authority must end. Structural layers within the Deterministic Structural Core must remain mechanically verifiable and externally governable. AI may augment bounded domains—transformation suggestion, anomaly detection, optimization—provided that deterministic validation gates, circuit breakers, and rollback mechanisms remain intact. In this architecture, AI functions as a co-processor within engineered boundaries, not as a structural authority.

These four dimensions—lifecycle discipline, semantic elevation, system representation, and bounded AI augmentation—do not operate independently. They reinforce one another. Lifecycle segmentation isolates responsibility. Semantic elevation preserves transparency across those boundaries. System representation formalizes control. AI boundary design ensures that probabilistic intelligence enhances rather than destabilizes structural invariants. When synthesized, they form a coherent infrastructural methodology.

Chapters four through nine translated this methodology into construction practice. Data modeling was reframed as canonical backbone engineering rather than report shaping. Lineage became an intrinsic state rather than inferred documentation. Data quality evolved into reliability engineering, complete with executable contracts and containment mechanisms. Governance and security were expressed as queryable control layers rather than static policies. Orchestration migrated from episodic workflow tooling to a declarative control plane. Consumption transformed from dashboard production into intelligent interface design. Each component was treated not as a feature, but as a subsystem within a regulated grid.

What emerges from this synthesis is a new understanding of data infrastructure maturity. Infrastructure maturity is not measured by the number of tools deployed, the volume of data stored, or the sophistication of analytics produced. It is measured by the degree to which uncertainty is bounded, lineage is reconstructable, semantics are stable, and evolution is possible without structural collapse. A mature Data Grid behaves less like a collection of pipelines and more like a regulated network. It operates continuously. It isolates faults. It preserves memory. It exposes state. It evolves without rewriting its foundations.

The implications extend beyond architecture into organizational design. When data becomes infrastructure, engineers transition from building isolated artifacts to defining system rules and boundaries. Governance becomes executable. Reliability becomes measurable. Decision-making shifts from extracting reports to interacting with governed intelligence systems. Organizations that adopt infrastructure thinking gain compounding advantages: integration costs decrease, semantic reuse increases, AI deployment becomes safer, and systemic trust accumulates over time.

The future evolution of the Data Grid will not eliminate complexity. Instead, it will structure complexity. As AI systems grow more capable, as data volumes continue expanding, and as cross-organizational interoperability becomes necessary, the demand for deterministic structural cores will intensify. The grid must remain stable even as intelligent agents experiment at its edges. It must support continuous adaptation without surrendering auditability. It must permit probabilistic reasoning while preserving deterministic state representation.

This is why the Data Grid is not a transient architectural pattern. It is the next evolutionary expression of infrastructure engineering in a software-defined world. It transfers principles from electrical grids, distributed systems, control theory, and reliability engineering into the domain of data. It insists that infrastructure discipline precedes intelligent autonomy. It establishes that scalable intelligence requires structured containment. In closing, we return to the proposition introduced at the beginning of this book. Technology transforms industries, but infrastructure determines whether transformation endures. The AI era will not be defined solely by the power of models. It will be defined by whether organizations succeed in constructing soft infrastructure capable of sustaining intelligence at scale. The Data Grid is the engineering blueprint for that construction. It formalizes lifecycle continuity, semantic self-description, deterministic system representation, and explicitly engineered AI boundaries. It transforms data from fragmented artifacts into regulated flow. It establishes data infrastructure as a disciplined engineering domain rather than a collection of loosely coupled tools.

The purpose of this book has been to articulate that doctrine. The task that remains belongs to the reader: to build systems that do not merely process data, but sustain intelligence. That is the promise—and the responsibility—of the Data Grid.